Hilarious Hunting, Camp and Fishing Stories
Vol. 5

By: The U.P. Rabbit
Robert R. Hruska

Hilarious Hunting, Camp and Fishing Stories
(A U.P. SEQUEL, VOL. 5)

First Edition: 2006
Copyright © 2006
ISBN # 0-9668265-4-X

Published by
McNaughton & Gunn, Inc.
960 Woodlawn Drive
Saline, Michigan 48176

All inquires should be addressed to:
Robert R. Hruska, Author
140 S. Birch Avenue
Gillett, Wisconsin 54124
Telephone: (920) 855-2996

Illustrations by:
Michael Delbridge

Dedication

"To all of my hunting and fishing partners over the years…I feel enriched and privileged from having all of those experiences with you."

Table of Contents

GOOD OLD DAYS   CH. I

ILLUSTRATIONS BY
MIKE DELBRIDGE

Chapter 1

The Good Old Days of Hunting?

My brother and I love to hunt. We were just learning about it from our Dad who just recently started hunting himself. He hunted before we did, so that made him the expert. We very seldom questioned any tips that he passed down to us. We may have looked back at him a little strange sometimes but we never questioned him.

At this time he had an older Dodge car with bald tires. A trip up to the camp was an ordeal and an experience. Dad always seemed to be listening for a blow-out so he could slam on the breaks quickly. It seemed that most people had bald tires during the war years.

Those slow-speed trips seemed like very long trips. We boys sat in the back seat and always thought up some activity to pass the time. The old "tire sizzling" trick worked if we didn't use it too often. As we were riding slowly, Dad always listened for some type of expected tire action. So we'd sit in the back seat and make a ZZZZZZZ zzzzzzzzzz ZZZZZZZZZZZ sound with our mouth like air leaking out of a tire. He'd slow up more and listen. We'd then quit until he felt there was no problem. Then we'd start sizzling again but change the pitch higher and lower. He'd watch the road; look quickly into the back seat checking if it was US making that sound or was it real?

1

We had enough flats that we had that sound down perfect. Experience taught us when to quit that little game and to think of something else.

Dad did lay out some good deer drives that we used for years. Most of them we had to later abandon because different people bought the land that the drives were on. Another reason, as we got older, it was a lot easier to find good deer crossings and let them come to you. All of our drives had names. The Triangle Drive, the Jacket Drive (someone had left a jacket hanging in a tree crutch and it stayed there for years), the Hardwoods Drive, the Chocolate Drop Drive and the Spruce Swamp Drive. When a drive name was mentioned, we all knew where to post it and how to drive it out.

Arriving at camp, Dad would make one of his famous meals. A ring of small bologna and a can of beans, or, some eggs boiled in the tea kettle on the wood stove. Depending on how long they boiled, we either had loose, soft boiled eggs or hard boiled eggs. Another meal was what my brother and I affectionately called, "Gruel". Dad would tell us that it was oatmeal. We learned to love it when my mother came to camp with us and did the cooking.

Then there was the time when Dad was going to show us a new post he had made in the middle of an 80 acre cedar swamp. He explained that it was a high spot in the middle of the swamp where deer crossed and laid down there from the signs that he observed. He filled a burlap sack ½ full of apples (about a bushel) and we started off into that swamp looking for this high spot somewhere in the middle.

The swamp had about a foot of snow in it. No trails from any logging to walk on or get a direction bearing from. The cedar all looked alike. After we all took a turn carrying that bag of apples, Dad stopped and said, "I do believe that we're lost, boys." We started to figure to what advantages were on our side. One, we had a lot of daylight. Then, brother Bill said, "Do you have your compass?" "No," answered Dad. "Where is it?" countered Bill. "Don't know, lost it." shrugged Dad. "Did you tell Grandpa that you lost his compass?" "Nope, I'll square it away with him and give him some cigarettes."(At that time, no one knew that cigarettes were 'cancer sticks').

Bill was muttering to himself, "Lost the compass and now lost us." "What did you say?" asked Dad, "Oh, just said, we sure got a lot of apples to eat if we want to." "Keep the apples, we might find that spot yet." countered Dad. He said, "Let's see, moss always grows on the north side of trees." I said, "Here's some with moss growing on all sides of the trees." "Look for some with it growing on only one side." he said.

Bill, thinking out loud, said, "Red sky in the morning, sailor take warning, red sky at night, sailor's delight." "What's that got to do with us being lost out here?" Dad asked. "Nothing." Bill said, "It just came to me." Dad, trying to look like the fearless leader and a bit disgusted, said, "Let Bill carry the apples for a while."

We march on, not willing to admit that some Trolls came at night and moved that choice high spot somewhere else in the swamp. As we walked, we scared up a lot of snowshoe rabbits. They seemed to be running all around

3

us. Dad said, "Don't shoot any rabbits. It's just something more to carry." "What if we stay lost all night?" Bill asked. "Shoot some rabbits." Dad countered.

We easily shot two rabbits and now carried them with us. As I thought of eating FRESH rabbit over a roasting fire (Thank God Dad smoked, he always had matches) that bologna and beans back at camp was sounding pretty good.

Then a miracle happened. We came to an old foundation from a house and remnants of a road leading away from it. Dad said, "It's surprising what you find in a cedar swamp." Bill commented," I think we've been in hardwoods lately and we've been walking uphill." "See how easy it is to get mixed up? Let this be a lesson to you. Always take a compass with you." Dad answered.

Taking the road, we made our way out to the main gravel road. We learned many things about the woods and hunting with Dad on that trip. Never go into strange woods without a compass. Never carry a bushel of apples around in a cedar swamp, and never let Dad rest his 12 gauge shotgun on your shoulder for a better aim when he shoots at a rabbit. Bill's ears were ringing for an hour later. And ....never, never complain about little bologna and beans again. They beat blood-dripping, fresh rabbit any day.

Dad leaned back on his chair at the camp table, "A little brisk walk like that really is good for the appetite and should make you sleep good." Bill had his head down on the table asleep already. The hot wood heat in the camp compared to the cold "swamp death-march" that we just finished made him sleep like a baby. I noticed that he

4

had one hand around his allotted piece of little bologna so no one would take it. Bologna beat two hour old rabbit anytime.

Aino & Toivo Go Hunting

Two hunters were dragging their dead deer back to their car. Another hunter approached pulling his along too.

"Hey, I don't want to tell you how to do something... but I can tell you that it's much easier if you drag the deer in the other direction. Then the antlers won't dig into the ground."

After the third hunter left, the two decided to try it.

A little while later one hunter said to the other, "You know, that guy was right. This is a lot easier!"

"Yeah, but we're getting farther from the truck," the other added.

CATS DON'T CH 2
BARK

Chapter 2

Cats Don't Bark

Our two boys were of the age where they should have a pet. As my wife said, "They NEED a pet. It will keep them from picking on each other." She was right, of course. We drove a Volkswagen Rabbit at this time. I proudly bragged about getting 55 miles to the gallon of gas, never mind that the two kids in the back seat had their heads between their pulled-up knees for room.

It was a car built for two people in the front seats and a few grocery bags in the back. Our boys displaced more room than grocery bags and naturally then, would pick on each other for a little more space if nothing else. The thing that saved both of them from any real harm was that there wasn't enough room back there to really fade back and land a REAL punch.

My wife, Barb, said, "Those people in Germany must be smaller people to fit into a back seat of a Volkswagen." Six years later, we went to Germany for two weeks to visit our oldest son who was in the service and his wife. I couldn't help but notice the number of Volkswagens on the road there. Most all of them had 2-3 kids in the back seat. The adults were shouting something in German that didn't sound too nice. The father was driving and shaking his fist in the back seat. The mother, on the passenger's side, was holding her hands on her ears. It looked like the Germans had the same problem. 55 miles to the gallon but no space.

Now how does this affect us in getting a dog? As a family, we go to our camp almost every weekend of the year. There's fishing, hunting, hiking, trees to climb, birds of flush, and space. A place to watch nature, use your imagination and fresh air.

The problem was how do you fit a dog into our already overloaded car? There was no way. If we left the dog home on weekends, it would naturally bark constantly and make the neighbors hostile again. If you left it in the house by itself, it would make a mess relieving itself wherever, as dogs do.

A cat seemed to be a good answer. A cat could be a loving pet, teach warmth and be fun to play with. Cats were also natural hunters. Think of the mice, chipmunks and things that they catch. They also don't bark for hours on end and bother the neighbors. It would also go into a litter box when it had the urge rather than anywhere in the house. At first, it was a hard sell, but, both boys realized that there was no room in the car to transport a dog on weekends. A cat would be O.K. Besides, they felt that they could teach the cat to hunt with them. Bobcats and tigers are hunters, aren't they? So, we got a cat. A nice cat from a friendly farmer that lived close by... for free.

I should have suspected something when he was on his knees thanking us for taking it. It seemed that the mother cat would have a new litter almost every 9 months. He said, "I can't keep up with them. There getting to be so many. Can't even feed all of them. I spend hours

7

looking for that mother cat with my Remington persuader but she is smart and hides."

That cat looked like a fighter and probably would make a good hunter. It was every color of other cats within a 10 mile radius. Its nose looked broken and hung to one side, probably from fighting for its share of milk.

As we were talking, the hired hand came running and screaming out of the barn with a milk pail splashing. Two cats were biting and hanging onto him. They were trying to get to that milk. The farmer, not wanting us to give back the cat, with a smile said, "This breed of cat make good fighters and hunters. Your boys should have good luck hunting with YOUR cat."

My boys were smiling. They could see possibilities here. We thanked him and drove away with our new pet. I was smiling and thinking. IT WON'T BARK! My boys were both smiling. God only knows what THEY were thinking. My wife looked half frightened at it over her shoulder and wouldn't tell anyone what SHE was thinking.

Well, that cat did develop into a hunter and a real fighter. It developed a dislike for anyone other than the family members who came near the house. We had no idea that it could fight so viciously and quickly. It didn't bark but it would make an ungodly loud hissings sound seconds before it struck.

One time an insurance salesman came over to try and sell us more life insurance. We were gathered around the living room table, his stuff was spread out and he was saying, "If one of your loved one dies, you will want

8

more of this insurance to sustain you." I and the whole
family saw that cat (by now, the boys named him Killer)
slid under the table. We all subconsciously, tightened our
muscles ready to jump our legs back as Killer made his
loud hissing sound.

The salesman continued, "All you have to do is make this
small pay, pay, payyyyyyyyy......Killer hissed loudly,
we jumped, the salesman unfortunately was too relaxed,
didn't know, and couldn't jump away. His eyes opened
so wide, you'd swear they were going to pop out. He
looked when he saw all of us standing on our chairs. He
then started to slide slowly under the table. The hissing
was getting louder, almost like a stream, and that cat
wouldn't let go. He was doing a good job of shredding
the salesman's pant leg.

Remember, at this point, the salesman had no idea what
had a hold of him. He probably thought, "Do they keep a
pet alligator?"... What? Finally, he got a good grip on
the back of his chair and pulled himself free. He grabbed
his brief case full of unsigned insurance forms and ran for
the door. That cat was hissing so loud that it was ear
piercing. It was right behind him. He slammed the
screen door against the house as he leaped over the porch
railing. The cat stopped at the railing. Word must have
gotten out among the salesman as we don't even have
many telemarketers call on us anymore.

One weekend, we left that cat home alone in the house
when we went to the cabin. A burglar worked his way in
through an unlocked window. I really don't know what
happened between him and the cat but he didn't take
anything and left a big bag full of goodies that he took

from some other house. I could only guess, probably a peace offering to get back out alive.

The boys loved that cat. Not many people had killer cats. The other kids at school would tease them that they had a cat for a pet and not a macho dog like they had. Mine would smile and invite them over to "play or tease" the cat. After the first couple came over, Killer was well respected. If any neighborhood kids started any "rough housing", my boys would hiss loudly like Killer the cat. Those kids would either jump up on their chairs or the lucky ones ran for the door.

Killer wouldn't chase rabbits around in a circle so you could shoot one or point at a partridge when he saw one. But, if any wild game came within 10 feet of him, Killer had it. Once, I saw a male coyote sneak up on Killer by the camp. I heard that horrible, high pitched hiss from Killer and then saw that coyote painfully crying for help and running slowly into the woods. Killer was hanging between its back legs. It looked like he had it by the base of its tail. He made a good pet because, CATS DON'T BARK...BUT THEY HISS!

MOSQUITO JACK   CH.3

Chapter 3

Mosquito Jack

Everyone always called him Mosquito Jack because he was always slapping at himself and in a low voice would say, "Mosquito." as he slapped. Jack lived in a cedar swamp.

Jack was about 75 years old, built short, with longer legs than his body. The locals said that Jack got that way from carrying cedar posts out of the swamps on his shoulders all of his life in the woods. It kind of pushed down the top part of his body and bowed his legs.

He'd come to town about twice a week because he was lonely. He lived alone back in the woods. No one ever knew of any relatives that Jack had. A real loner.

Quiet natured, he'd go to the local restaurant and order coffee and sit and listen. Jack never seemed to have many friends. He'd sit and listen to whoever he thought was saying something interesting. For practical purposes after the first glance at him, you could easily forget he was even there.

The waitresses would "kid" him that one of them was going to marry him and get all his money. Jack would say, "You're not getting' MY money!" I asked the waitress if he HAD money. She explained, "Look, if he

11

did, don't you think he'd get a better pickup truck or get his teeth fixed? Every once in a while, he spits out a tooth when he's eating. He's got that 'long-in-the-tooth' disease."

I looked harder at him and his mouth WAS starting to look like a Jack-O-Lantern. He was rolling his tongue around in his mouth against his teeth. Probably wondering how long he could still eat corn on the cob. It was raining hard this week, when I was up to my camp. That's a good enough excuse to go into town and eat breakfast at the restaurant. A time to talk to some of the "good ole boys."

I walked in and at a small table by himself sat Jack. He had on some rain gear, his sorrel boots and a greasy cap that, I'm sure, by now, was waterproof. His boots were only laced up ½ way because it wasn't really that cold yet. Jack was sitting and listening, as this was his routine. No one really spent time visiting with him other than a "How you doing, Jack?" and kept walking by. He'd look up with that "every-other-tooth" grin and say nothing.

It was raining harder outside now, so everyone in that restaurant was sitting longer. No reason to go out and maybe, you'd pick up a little news. Suddenly, something highly unusual happened! A stranger sat at Jack's table across from him. He must have introduced himself and then started the conversation.

"I've heard that you live alone and own a substantial land holding worth some top dollar." "Have I got a good deal for YOU!" He was selling or trying to sell, some life insurance. Jack was looking back kind of blank at him,

12

trying figure out why he was talking to him and probably, what that "substantial" meant.

"I've got a deal just made for someone like you." The guy then could sense that he wasn't getting through to Jack. He tried a different approach, "You know, you're not going to live forever. You could die soon." Jack narrowed his eyes and stared hard at the stranger. "What do you now about me dying?" Jack asked suspiciously.

The salesman said, "Well, it's got to happen. Don't you want to go see the Lord?" Jack quietly said, "I don't want anyone crowding me on that......" Then the salesman tried to reach him by evaluating his assets to write up a plan.

"How much Social Security do you get per month?" Jack looked at him and half standing up, said, "So you found out about that, did you? I figured some government blood hound would visit me on that someday. Just because I didn't pay into it, now you want to take it away…" Jack was getting this for the last five years. He lived with the fear that someone would swoop in one day and cut it off on him.

After all these years, Jack felt that they probably thought he was dead but kept paying it anyway. After all, the government does some odd things.

The salesman now smiling at Jack, said, "I'll figure out a nice life insurance policy for you that you can afford on Social Security." Jack got up and went into the restroom. He came out about 20 minutes later, hoping the guy would be gone.

13

The friendly salesman realized quickly, that he wasn't making sales headway here. He said to Jack, "Why don't I come to your house tonight and finish this with you?" Is there anyone else at home with you?" Jack told him only his dog and it's a bitter. The guy understood Jack to say it was a "Buyer." "I never heard of a dog like that."

Jack slowly smiled and said, "Come on out. I'll have the dog in the house so you can see him up real close. So you found out about my Social Security, did you? Sure....come on over tonight. Me and "Buyer" (Jack smiled from ear to ear) will be waiting for you......"

The local guys saw Jack in the restaurant the next day. "What happened out at your house, Jack with that stranger?" Jack looked down into his coffee, smiled and said, "He didn't stay too long......"

CHANGE OF SEASONS

Chapter 4

Change of Seasons...Fishing to Deer Hunting

Four of us from our camp went on a September week-long fishing trip to Canada. For us, this is an annual trip to catch some very big brook trout and it starts to prepare us for deer season. Why are these similar? Well, the September trip to remote Canada has a touch of cooler than normal feeling in the air and it's the start of the fall cold, cold winds, and adventure.

We fly-in to a lake that has no roads near it, or other fishermen for at least 50 miles. Two weeks after we leave that camp, moose hunters have it rented for hunting. Most of that hunting is done at the waters edge as a dead moose is almost impossible to carry out of the woods.

We did catch a lot of nice-sized trout and had some good fish fries. Whenever you have to cut a brook trout into 3 pieces just to fit it into an average-sized fry pan, you know you have caught big fish.

This year, one of our boats sank to the bottom while tied up to the dock. The dock is a floating raft tied to the shore. There are so many big rocks off shore that you have to dock out past them. There were gale type winds blowing that night. Trees were bending way over and you could hear some cracking. The wave action on the

15

water must have become so great that they were breaking over the back of the boat, filled it, in time, with water. We spent a 1/2 day getting it back into working shape to fish again.

Jerry took a walk down the beach (a walk is approximately 75 yards then it has impassable underbrush growing out into the water) and saw very fresh moose tracks within 50 yards from where we had the boat docked.

Bill took the walk about 2 hours later. He saw the moose tracks AND one set of BLACK BEAR TRACKS only about 40 yards from the boat. I placed both of my hands along with 3 inch claw prints in the moist beach sand. Carl estimated that the bear was over 400 pounds. Carl is an old bear hunter from way back. He said, "Be sure no one leaves any garbage or fish heads around. We don't want to give it an excuse to hang around."

Now, that was pretty good motivation to run a clean camp. We hoped that we didn't even SEE that one, even on a distant shore. The best weapon that we had was a small ax for splitting firewood. We had an outdoor toilet, not too close to camp, and may need it in the dark.

We were all doing well until after we finished our last big fish fry. We also had made 5 lbs of American fries, fried liberally in cooking oil. Everything went down well with everyone. Content fishermen with a wonderful meal.

It was about 45° that night after lights out and we were all in our bunks. Suddenly I saw a flashlight shine on the inside wall, the ceiling and the floor. Then, I heard someone running across the floor and out the door. I got up and checked. Here was Shank sitting on a 5 gallon pail on the porch "doing his thing," He said, "I'm sorry but I couldn't make it to the outhouse." As we were using that pail to haul lake water up to the camp, I said to Shank, "Now, I wonder WHO ELSE might have used that pail for that before we ever came here?"

That was known thereafter, as, "The night Shank slid out of bed because he ate too much grease."

Deer Hunting

These same guys are now preparing all of the necessities to go deer hunting out of Bob's camp in Lake Township, Menominee County. We checked the deer blinds over for repairs. The tar paper either blew off or was pulled off the front of Wayne's blind (now used by Carl). We'll fix that next weekend when we bring up those supplies.

On the plus side, there are now THREE main deer trails intersecting in front of that blind. Last year, there was only one. The other blinds still look good with a lot of deer sign. Looks like this should be a good year. Bill said, "We'll have to place a 5 gallon pail on the porch. Shank seems partial to those 5 gallon pails."

"There's really a lot of deer tracks and sign by my blind this year coming out of the cedar swamp," Carl said, "Did anyone notice the wolf tracks in the sand around there? Must be a few wolves around there." Bill told him, "Why do you think the newest guy was given a deer blind with such good deer sign? Sure there's wolves around there. Footprints as big as your hand. You can imagine

17

the size that those wolves must be. You're not allowed to
shoot them either, unless they're attacking you."

Carl thought that over for a while and then said, "What
does attacking mean? Do they have to have a hold of
you?" Bill said, "If they have a hold of you, we call that
the "feeding stage." "Whatever you do, don't fall asleep
in that post."

Carl looked around the table at everyone. He's been
through this before. In fact, he started some of these
stories himself at times. This is all part of the deer
season. Preparations, stories, and building up
expectations.

With the right hunting camp partners, getting the buck is
only part of a successful season. Good luck with your
hunt and remember, SHOOT STRAIGHT!

Brother Bill with a Canadian "Brook Trout" 16 ½ long.
A real scrapper!

CHAPTER #5

DEER CAMP LIFE

Chapter 5

Deer Camp Life – Last Season

Yes, for most deer camps, this is the highlight of the hunt. The camp life………..everyone likes to get a buck but the camp life seems to make the most memories until the next deer season.

This is the second Monday of the season and I'm the first one back in the camp. Its 12:00 noon and I was out there since 6:30 a.m. It is just beginning to snow here now, a windy, blowing snow. The kind that makes deer settle in a swamp, marsh, or under some thick evergreen trees.

I saw one doe at 10:30 a.m. She came partly to my bait pile but kept one foot in the swamp for a quick get-a-way. They are really "spooked" now because of the shots in the woods and the white snow background.

I know that there still is a nice "racker" by my deer blind. I saw it last week Friday but couldn't get even a snapshot of it. I'd guess that it was between a 10 to 12 pointer. But then, I'm a fisherman too, and we seem to always add on a few inches when a big one gets away.

The first day at camp, we had two small deer (fawns) walking all around the camp and looking in the kitchen window. That window is about waist high on an adult person. I don't believe that anyone shot them, but, they too, seemed to have now found a hole to hide into for the rest of the season.

Our camp had three hunters for the first three days. We got two nice spike-horns and a high-horned fork-horn. Three for three in two days. The does are really plentiful this year too. Does anyone remember the years when you could get a "camp deer" to eat at camp? I'm looking around the kitchen now, I see a big pot of Chili, a frozen container (must be two gallons) of chicken boyah, a sauerkraut hot dish that we have been eating for four days now. The guys really love it and call it "Vic's favorite." He hunted with us previously and we had some kind of a marathon by eating that same hot dish for five days in a row. Vic didn't like it and made it known. The cook kept serving venison stew that is three days old now. It's almost a tradition, but Dave brings up his apple pie. Another fixes the crust and bakes it. Who said that men can't cook?

A few strange things have been happening up here lately. Normally, during mating season, the bucks chase the does around for breeding purposes. We couldn't help but notice that up here, the does chase the bucks around for mating. Sometimes there are 4-5 does running after one poor buck at the same time. Dave was watching that, smiled, and said, "When I die, that's the way I want to go – It must be something in the water up here......"

We told that story one night at the Chip-In Casino to a few Lower Michigan "city hunters". They listened like they just heard a deeply kept secret. One said seriously, "I never heard of that before." Bill told them, "I'll bet you bought a lot of buck lure to lure in a buck didn't you?

Throw all of it away and buy doe lure. That will help
you to get a nice buck."
The blackjack dealer, a young girl, was laughing
inwardly and had tears coming down her cheeks. She
must have been a hunter too, but didn't want to change
our story for these L.P. boys who seemed to appreciate
any good advice that we gave them.

The following is a true story of that fork-horn that we
shot: It was facing Carl and it was shot in its front
shoulder. The bullet passed through the total deer (the
long way) and we never touched any meat or stomach
intestines. But when we lifted its tail to clean it, the spent
bullet just fell out from under its tail and onto the ground.
That bullet passed through the entire deer's body, never
touching either hind quarter but came out perfectly
through the you-know-where.

One camp member arrived later. He was noticeably
serious, dishearten, because he now reached the mature
age of having a lot of aches and pains and things wrong
with his heart. He was feeling sorry for himself and had
a few brews. A few more brews and listening to him, we
got feeling sorry for him too and joined him with a few.

After about an hour of this, he said, "Guys, I went to a
specialist and he told me that I got so many things wrong
with me. I've got Diabetes, high blood pressure,
rutabagas, and some kind of gas problems (we didn't
need to have a specialist tell us about the gas problem.
We could have saved him a trip to the doctor on that
one.)

By now, he was feeling no pain. He said, "Anyone of
these could be killers." Carl said, "You got rutabagas?

(Our friend Shank, didn't realize that he included that one and still didn't), "Pills, all kinds of pills."

Carl later told the group, "Guys, I'm not going to put on any deodorant until I shoot a buck. I think they can smell that deodorant." Bill sniffed the air, "I sure hope you get that buck soon."

Bill, later, went to his son-in-law's camp and got into a card game. I should first tell you, this camp is made up of hell raisers, jokers, anything for a laugh bunch of jolly people. Bill told us about the card game, "I never saw so much cheating in all my life. They were using signals almost like a 3rd base coach does," (pass one hand over the heart, etc) He said, "When they all got away from the table, I saw cards on the floor from someone 'adjusting' their hand."

As I mentioned before, we went to the Chip-In Casino on Monday night. They had a Big Buck Contest in progress when we arrived. The outside of the casino on one side was lit up like the inside of a building. It looked like a funeral procession of pickup trucks lined up waiting to show who had the biggest deer and set of horns.

One party with a huge buck had the deer's antlers chained to their pickup and locked to the side of it. Channel 6 TV from Marquette was interviewing hunters. The Escanaba radio station was also interviewing as many as they could. I talked on the radio interview and told about our success in Lake Township, Menominee County by our camp.

One local old-timer who told us he was only shooting 8-pointers or better (he got his picture in the Menominee

Co. Journal last year on shooting an 8-pointer) said, "I think those bucks unscrewed their horns after the first day and hid them under a stump. All I see is does."

I can now see a blaze orange cap coming into camp from our back road. It's probably Carl as that is his direction. WE should hear some kind of deer story from that post. Carl just came in, smiled and said, "I go to camp and my wife goes Christmas shopping. What a nice trade-off."

Tuesday, the second week of the season, its 26° and the snow looks permanent now and is about ½ inch deep. Good tracking snow for whoever will be hunting in the cold. We've got a nice wood fire going in the heater and are enjoying life inside of our deer camp. Its 26° outside and 78° inside (no wonder we feel cold when we get back home with the controlled heat for a house furnace.)

The buck pole is full. It doesn't get any better than this.............

COYOTES-NOT NICE

Ch 6

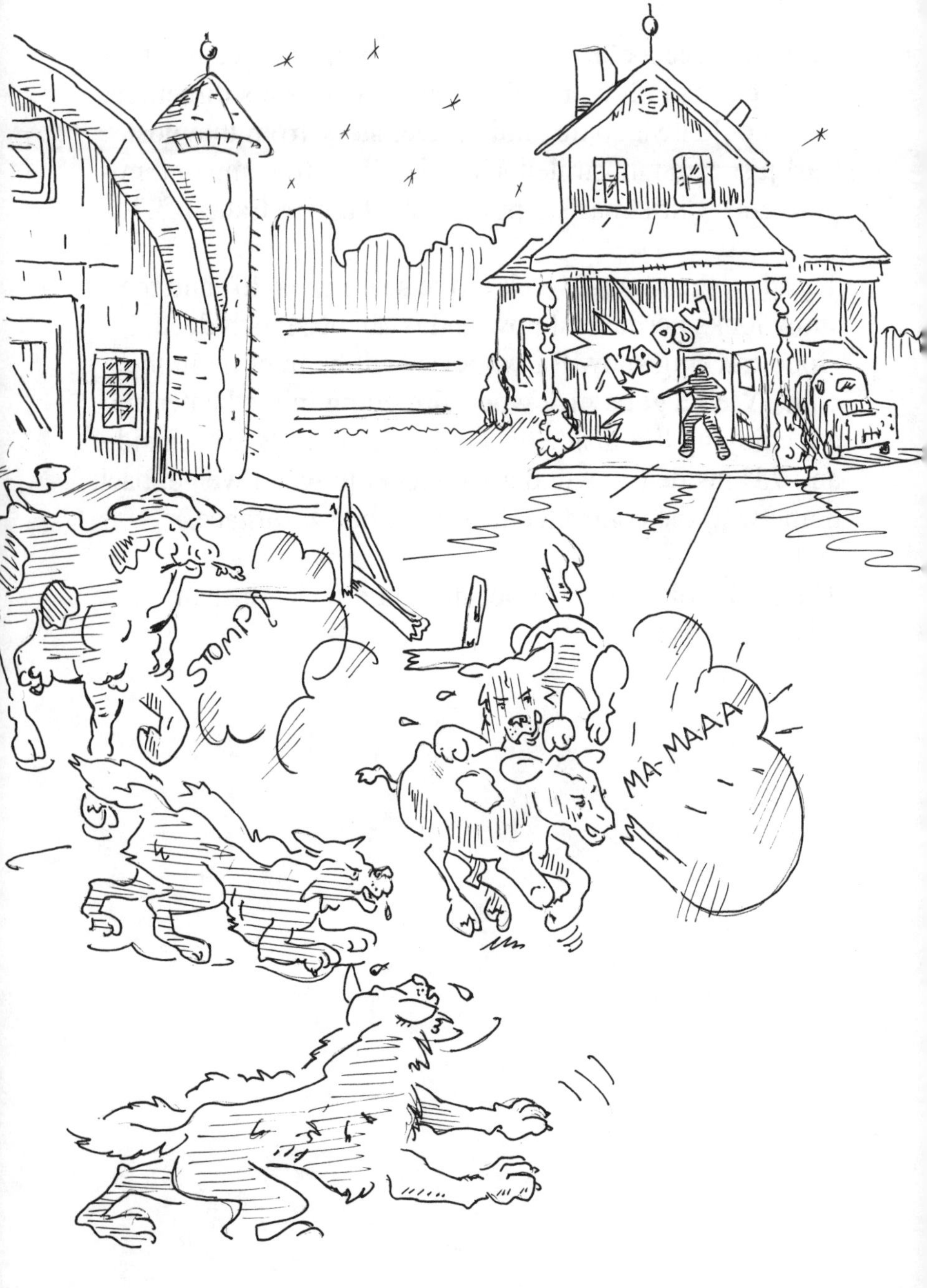

Chapter 6

Coyotes Are Not Nice Guys

Coyotes don't bother anyone. They just eat mice,
rabbits, and maybe an occasional partridge. If you
believe that, you should spend some time talking with a
Menominee farmer, John Lepianka. John's farm is
located about 17 miles north of Menominee and south of
Stephenson. Like any successful farmer today, he knows
what its like to work hard and to mange his resources
wisely.

A newborn calf is a natural money resource for a farmer.
A calf born about now, and fed until fall will grow and
probably bring $400.00 into the farm's cash flow.

Three weeks ago, John came in from his barnyard
smiling and told his wife, Judi, "That black angus calf
was just born. It's laying about 20 feet from the barn and
the mother is licking it clean right now."

They could see it from the kitchen window so they sat
down at the kitchen table and had their morning coffee.
They had a good view of the barnyard and of the mother
cow and the newborn calf. The calf was still lying on the
ground. Being only about 3 hours old, that calf could
only lift its head up and wait until it gained more
strength.

John was smiling. A black angus was something special. It was worth more than your average calf. Suddenly, a strange thing happened! A huge coyote ran out of the woods and bolted toward the newborn calf. "It happened so fast," John said, "You couldn't do anything about it." That coyote made a bee-line for the calf, snarled at the cow and turned onto the calf.

It bit the calf on its nose with a 'snapping turtles' grip. It then ripped open the calf's belly as quickly as any hunter's knife could open up a deer. Of course, the deer hunter completely kills the deer first. It then bit the intestines and started to pull them out to eat. The cow, with the natural mother's instinct, bellowed and charged the coyote. That coyote skillfully dodged the cow and darted in and bit the cow's nose and the cow's teats, it's most sensitive and hurtful places where the cow was helpless.

In pain, the cow jumped away to protect herself. By now, John was out the kitchen door with his .30/30 in his hand. The coyote saw him immediately and ran quickly back into the woods. John then checked the calf and saw that it was a goner. Its belly was ripped open and the animal was gasping its last. (This was a 3 to 4 hour old animal.)

The ever-protective mother came over to chase him away. He figured that he'd leave them alone for awhile and he went back into the house. They were finishing their coffee and John said, "Well, we're going to be about $400.00 poorer this fall because of that coyote." Within 10 minutes time, that coyote came running back for seconds. It again chased away the mother cow and began eating the innards from that newborn calf."

"This time, I was ready for him," said John. "I picked up my .30/30 deer rifle with the scope on it, took a resting aim on the door frame and had time for only one shot. I hit him well in the front shoulders. There was no time for a follow-up shot. That thing tried to run back again into the woods but made it only about 30 feet and died."

He said that the coyote was also eating the toes off of the new calf. "After we took pictures, the first thing I did was to take it into the DNR station in Stephenson, showed them the evidence, and explained what happened." They said that I was well in my legal rights to shoot it from what it was doing. They took their own pictures from different angles of both animals and explained that a coyote or wolf can smell a newborn calf being born from a good 40 acres away. There is some type of distinct smell that they can pick up even at that distance."

The DNR will pay him $100.00 restitution, 'If the state can come up with the 100 bucks.' That is only a small part of what it would have sold for in the fall. (The wild coyotes, timber wolves, and bear are property of the state.)

This farm is also periodically bothered by bear. They will angle as close to the barn as they can looking for a meal.

John is an annual deer hunter like most U.P. residences are. He gets a buck every year and is a very good shot. He's got keen eyes that seem piercing when he looks at you. His vision is greater than 20/20. The kind of eye sight that the Air Force likes for its pilots to have......Hell, anyone who can hit a coyote with a .30/30 from a distance, has to be a good shot. He said that he shoots at anywhere from 3 to 10 bear a year. He shoots to scare them away from his farm. "After zinging a .30/30 shell past their heads, they get the idea and leave quickly."

John said, "You know, a farmer today, has to be pretty tough with these wild animals. I've got eagles circling over at times, to pick up a chicken; weasels, mink, skunks, who are trying to get into the chicken coop; fox, wolves, and coyotes trying to pick off any animal that they can, and deer and bear eating my corn."

Most people only see a coyote occasionally, traveling across a highway. But don't forget, they are
REAL KILLERS!

BEAR HUNTING

Chapter 7

Bear Hunting and the Relation

It was no secret that in the Hermansville and Conard area, there were more bear this year than one area deserves. Those bear pulled down bird feeders to get at the corn, tore doors off of storage sheds where the 'deer corn' was stored. The bear could be expected to be seen walking anywhere in the area, and frightened housewives half to death when they went out to the clothes lines and met a bear around the corner of the house.

Charlie, who lives in that area, told me that his wife screamed so loud when she encountered a bear around the corner of the house that it turned and ran away on its hind legs while covering its ears with its front paws. "A healthy and frightened woman has an ungodly powerful scream," said Charlie.

My relatives have a nice camp in the Conard area. The camp is about 5 miles off of US 2 down a single lane road. Road hunters and a few bear hunters also come down this road at times. Those bear hunters up there are not necessarily local people.

My sister-in-law, Donna, told me this story as we were visiting their camp. She said, "You wanted to hear about the bear hunters around here?" As she was talking, she moved to look down the road out the window. Her eyes were wide open. Wider than normal. She looked a little frightened and even shaken although she as secure in her own cabin.

"Some of them are really wild…Two weeks ago, on a nice peaceful weekend, John and I were walking down that single lane road looking at all of the peaceful scenery and expecting to see some deer or a partridge.

All of a sudden, we heard this loud, and I mean LOUD pickup truck come roaring around a corner. This was a bear hunter. You would have had to almost see this to believe it. The truck was old, beat up, and noisy. There was a big, blue tick hound chained up on the truck's hood looking ahead and hanging on for dear life.

His chain around his neck was attached to a hole in the hood so that the dog could sit up and I suppose, smell for bear as they were moving. Once in a while, they'd hit a pothole at that fast speed. The dog would fly off the hood as far as the chain would allow, howl like a hound, swing in a half circle and claw his way back onto the hood of the truck. The truck hood was all scraped clean of paint where that dog must have done that circle many times before.

It spread its legs and clung to the truck hood wherever a big dent made a foothold for it. It looked ½ crazed and hoped it would see or smell a bear soon so its owner would release it for the chase.

The driver didn't look much different from the dog. He had on a greasy, brown cap, a broad smile with a few spaced teeth missing. It seemed like he was looking out of all three windows at the same time and still trying to stay on the road. This was no ordinary man. He had a two-way radio in one hand and I suppose, was communicating with other hunters as they checked out this land section.

She said, "That dog knew he wasn't going to get any sympathy from anyone by the way that he felt around for the front bumper with his feet when he swung down off of the hood. He'd then push off of the bumper and pulled himself back onto the hood."

All this time, the truck was bouncing in and out of potholes and tearing down the road at a high rate of speed. He slammed on the brakes when he got in line with us. Road dust and gravel were flying everywhere. "See any 'Bar?' he asked. John said, "Bar? Oh, you mean, bear. Sure, three this morning about 10 miles away from here, down the road." John figured he would move this character away from his camp.

"Your dog seems to be having a rough ride," John said. "Yeah," the hunter explained, "I'll have to unfasten him and put Daisy up there. Daisy is in the back and rides up there better." He just mentioned Daisy and the dog in the back of the box started to howl mournfully. Like someone was twisting her tail, trying to pull her tooth. "Who said dogs don't understand what you're going to do," John whispered to his wife, Donna.

It sounded like Daisy wanted no part of that truck's hood. The driver said, "The dogs do OK on the hood if I drive real fast. Then, they don't get a chance to think. A thinking dog is a frightened bear hunting dog. If I go fast, they concentrate on hanging on and don't have time to do much thinking." "These dogs are well-trained,

WELL-TRAINED. They take the brunt of the beating when we corner a bear. Just think. If it wasn't for these dogs, we'd take that beating." Both of the dogs seemed to look at him at the same time.

"If you ever have a 'bar' that needs a little taming, I'll give you my card. Call me and I'll bring my whole crew in here." He pulled out a dirty, greasy card that was hard to read.

"Charlie, do you read me?" "Hey," Charlie said. "I'm getting a call. They spotted a track on the next crossroad. Got to go. Watch for the flying gravel," and he was off. The dog on the hood was lying on his belly, hanging onto the hood ornament with his two front paws and trying to grip the hood with his hind feet. It was staring straight ahead and its tail was straight back.

A man wakes up one morning to find a bear on his roof. So he looks in the yellow pages and sure enough, there's an ad for "Bear Removers." He calls the number, and the bear remover says he'll be over in 30 minutes.

The bear remover arrives, and gets out of his van. He's got a ladder, a baseball bat, a shotgun and a mean old pit bull.

"What are you going to do," the homeowner asks?

"I'm going to put this ladder up against the roof, then I'm going to go up there and knock the bear off the roof with this baseball bat. When the bear falls off, the pit bull is trained to grab his testicles and not let go. The bear will then be subdued enough for me to put him in the cage in the back of the van."

He hands the shotgun to the homeowner.

"What's this for?" asks the homeowner.

"If the bear knocks me off the roof, shoot the dog".

31

TYPICAL U.P. DEER CAMP   CH.8

Chapter 8

A Typical U.P. Deer Hunting Camp Experience

The U.P. Rabbit's hunting camp. We have a mixed crew that comes together for November 15th. The U.P. Rabbit, with the help of his brother-in-law and two sons, Bill, Carl, his son, Dave did the necessary chores before season. We hunt very close to the camp as well as far away. We don't want to make any unnecessary noise around camp, like, chopping wood, piling it on the porch, and whatever else needs doing.

This year, we set up a "Tent Blind" called an "Outhouse Blind" on the package it came in. Its 6 1/2 feet tall and camouflaged so you have difficulty seeing it from 20 feet away. We set it up, set a chair inside of it, tied it down so it couldn't blow away and we had a new, very successful blind. It is waterproof and the group agreed 100% that it was well-worth the money.

The guys are always trying something new each year. Bill put on some of that "Buck in Heat" deer lure and went close to his wife to check her reaction. She said, "God, do YOU need a bath. It smells like someone peed on you." (So much for a duel purpose "dear" lure.)

Storytelling is always a big event in camp. You've got the exaggerated "great" shots explained from the successful hunters to whatever "sparks" another story. Carl was telling about the first day deer that he saw running through. "They must have been so full of corn that their bellies were bouncing on the ground as they ran like basketballs."

Dave said, "I had a harder time going deer hunting this year. I had to leave my wife $300.00 to go shopping to satisfy her." Bill shrugged and commented, "I was pretty close to the same thing. I had to give my wife $200.00 for the casino to keep her happy." Carl listened to this and then said, "I don't know why you guys spend all that money. All I did was when we were still in bed, I said, "What will it be Honey? Sex or do I go deer hunting?" She had her back to me and said, "Don't forget your long underwear."

Bob said, "After that one, Carl, when we ask you how the weather is outside, we'll have to go and recheck it ourselves." Carl came back with, "The second night of season, it was pitch black outside and I had to go relieve myself, I heard some loud crashing sounds coming from the swamp. Then, a loud bugling sound like a buck in heat. More crashing around, then, it was quiet. Dave came out and heard it too. He said it sounds like that buck hit a homerun." (He knows stuff like that.)

I took Carl over to my friend, Gene Duby's camp to show him what a real U.P. hunting camp looks like. There were about 15 guys there when we arrived. They were all part of this camp crew. About 12 out of the 15 were smoking in the camp. They could have preserved a deer for a week with all that smoke. As usual, there were

33

more guys than they had double bunks for. Some sleep in easy chairs. Gene said, "And some don't know if they slept or not."

Gene said, "I'll bet your camp is shooting spike horns. (Gene owns 8-10, 40's and they have regular private breeding grounds for big bucks.) Not to be outdone, Carl said, "We're only shooting spike horns on up to 10 pointers." After a tour of the camp we all wished each other good luck and we went to Brother Bill's camp. He invited us over for a couple of big meals. Homemade chili that would melt ice on the sidewalk at 20° below. Brats, beans and homemade apple pie. His wife, Dawn, was the camp cook and I never saw his camp kitchen so clean.

When Carl and I entered their camp, she was sweating and telling Bill to "quit firing up that wood heater already!" Then, when she was baking that tasty, homemade pie, the electric stove oven would go on and off. So, it cooked, stopped, cooked, stopped, etc. She asked Bill what was wrong with the stove. He looked at it for awhile then said, "It's not working right." She looked at him like only a wife who wants a meal to come out perfect can and said, "I married a genius."

Card playing began in earnest just after a big supper by the camp cook, Dawn (who had the prestige of being the only female in camp.) I don't know if that was a privilege or a curse? Brother Bill, Dawn's husband, came up with a lot of instant rules of behavior around his wife. "When Dawn goes to the outhouse, everyone stays inside." "When Dawn goes in the bedroom the bedroom curtain stays closed." "Nobody touches Dawn." He had a way of making us feel like we were all "back home." One of the members, I won't mention his name, won a huge, frozen, turkey at the casino near Escanaba two nights ago. The guys were after Camp Cook Dawn to "Cook it up." She said, "How can I cook it when the stove oven stays on for a minute and goes off for a minute?" The best answer I heard was from Carl. He said, "Turn the oven up twice as high and it can cook twice as fast when it's on." Bob said, "Take it back and maybe you can win a cooked one."

Some problems seem so easy to solve.

Our friend Dave, from Marinette, came up for opening day, stayed over night, and helped pull in a 6 pointer the next day. It was taken from the "Tent Blind". He comes up to share the camp experiences with us then returns to Wisconsin to open his camp when the Wisconsin season starts, next Saturday.

Father Tim from Engadine is my nephew and is a member of our hunting party. We wanted someone to shoot a doe to turn it into sausage. I asked Father Tim if he saw any does when he came in. "No," he said, "I only saw a mother deer and her two young ones." Right there, we new Father Tim wasn't about to shoot our "sausage doe."

I hope your season was as good as ours. We all filled early with our respectful bucks. Now, we have time to relax more in camp, play cards, and hear the camp cook, Dawn, say, "Don't even think about it!" when someone passes her closely in the small kitchen.

The good-natured stories and kidding is all part of the camp experience. We shot two spike horns and one 6-pointer in the first two days. Bill shot an old "moss back" on the third day. Temperatures were in the 50's each day of the first week. Hopefully, next week will be cooler and the deer will be more active. They seem to need a cold snap for their natural instinct for mating and breeding to take place. Carl argued on this. He said, "It has to do with the position of the moon." Someone said, "That's why Carl's wife pulls the bedroom curtain so the moon can't shine in."

All in all, the fresh air, thrill of the hunt, camp stories, respect of our fellow hunter's boundaries of their lands, good meals, and friendships are an unbeatable experience.

Chapter 9

Just Another U.P. Fish and Fisherman?

For anyone who thinks you have to go to Canada for really big fish, here's proof that the U.P. lunkers still are here.

My cousin, Gerald, thought that he'd try for a few pan fish, perch, or possibly a northern. He put his 14 foot boat in at the mouth of the Menominee River. October 28, 2004 was probably more suited for duck hunting than fishing. Cold, damp, and an overcast sky. Not many "fair weather fisherman" were out on a day like this.

"There were a few boats on the bay too, off at a distance. They left about noon and I was the only one still fishing out there," smiled Gerald. "Ducks were flying following the outer land points of shore, a pair of loons were working the area for a meal of fish, and other than that, it was quiet, cold, and getting lonely."

Gerald likes it that way. He likes the quiet, enjoys looking around and watching the beauty of the fall changes. Everything was at peace except for the cold and the damp. Someone else may have said, "It's a good day to stay inside."

Fishing with a light spinning rod and reel, the kind you'd use to fish pan fish with and have a lot of action on your pole, Gerald worked the area he knew for some pan fish. The waves were now getting a bit choppy and his boat started to bounce around in the water. Anyone with experience out on the bay knows wave conditions can change by the minute with wind, cold, and it seems a bit of orneriness. It's hard to hold a boat steady when you're fishing alone.

We were talking about fishing northern about a month ago. I told him that the biggest northern that I "almost got" was while trolling in Shaky Lakes (Menominee Co). I hooked one with a Dare Devil, got it alongside of the boat (it appeared to be about 30 inches long), I netted it, it kicked around in the net while still in the water and broke the side and bottom mesh out of the net and swam away like nothing happened. Since then, I replaced the nylon mesh. Well, he switched over to a jig and a good sized minnow. He was casting for a while to try to keep warm. Using a 6# test line with that "pan fish" fish pole and reel was a challenge. As long as a fisherman knows how to use the reel's "drag" properly, you can handle bigger fish, assuming they don't snap that light line.

The weather was getting colder rather than even staying the same. Waves were breaking on the water as small "white caps" were forming. He was thinking of leaving but wanted to stay a while longer as fishing normally improves when the water surface is rough and besides, he came a long way to fish here.

The area is such that you can dock anywhere along the shore and wait out a storm if you had to. A half hour of casting and no luck. He'd move periodically to fish new grounds. After one of these moves, he'd cast some more. On the third cast, he pulled back on the jig-bait and thought he had a snag. He pulled again on the line keeping in mind that it was only 6# test line and didn't want to break it.

After a few nudges and jerks to try and free it, HIS LINE STARTED TO MOVE! It took off and he had to run the motor to keep up with it. Then it stopped and went under his boat. This was about 2:00 p.m. He managed to get the fish to the top about four times. It broke the water, made a large splash, and went back down. He saw most of the fish and now knew that he had ONE BIG FISH! Gerald said, "I looked around the bay for some help but there was no one to holler to." He was on his own with a 14 foot bouncing boat, a fish larger than normal, on 6# test line. Then try as he would, he couldn't get that fish to come up again to net it. Gerald thought of all those *Outdoor* magazines that he ever read. He remembered one story where a fisherman in Canada lowered the anchor to the bottom near a fish to stir it up enough to bring it to the surface. He hesitated doing that as he could just see his fish getting tangled in the anchor rope. Finally, he tried it. IT WORKED! That big fish came up to the surface and close enough to the net. Gerald said that it looked like a submarine approaching. Now, how does one guy net such a huge fish, keep the boat steady, and not screw up? His landing net was made for an average sized walleye. This fish and that net would be like "trying to put 10 lbs of sand in a 5 gallon pail". He netted the head and up to the mid-point of the fish before it filled up the net. It gave a kick sideways and that helped bunch more of it into the net. "I pulled him and the net in over the side of the boat. It felt like landing a cement building block," said Gerald.

When it hit the side of the boat, it gave another kick with its tail and landed right in the bottom of the boat. That fish was almost as long as Gerald was tall. I asked, "How did you keep it from jumping back out?" "I jumped on it and forced its head underneath the middle seat. I held him that way for quite a while, then tied him securely with a rope to the middle seat and one side of the boat," explained Gerald. It took 21 minutes to get it into the boat. It measured 41 ½ inches long and weighed 18 pounds.

The fish was 41 ½ inches long or just 24 inches shorter than Gerald. The picture tells a lot about a successful catch. What did he do with such a huge fish? Because of its size, he had to drag it to his truck and again to the picnic table in his backyard. His wife, good natured, said, "Next time, how about bringing home a turkey or some steaks? I'm getting tired of fish."

He told me that he didn't have a wall left at home big enough to display this fish. (He already has deer mounts, bear, and other fish displayed on the walls), so he cut it up into chunks and froze it to eat later.

A "True Yooper," Gerald would rather eat it than just look at it. Who would believe that we still have fish like this in the good old Menominee area? Now, he's getting ready for the bow and arrow deer season, rifle season, and black powder season. To visit him during these seasons, one would have to be lucky and stumble onto his deer blind to find him. He said, "I have had the same deer blind for 43 years and shot 43 bucks there. I don't use any bait as that attracts a lot of does and fawns." He's got to be one of the last of the "Old Breed" sportsman.

Chapter 10

Deer Baiting Advice From The "Good Ole Boys"

I stopped into my favorite restaurant near my camp last weekend. There are always a few "good ole boys" in there having coffee and it seems, in need of company.

In a small town that's where you go for company without stopping at someone's house and that's where you hear the latest news. This last weekend, the place was half filled with "tourist hunters" (as they are called by the locals). They were all dressed in camouflaged clothes for turkey hunting.

Dick commented, "If that bunch didn't move at that corner table, you'd swear that was a pile of brush." The atmosphere with the local guys seemed to have a quiet mystic hanging over them. They were definitely waiting for something or for something to happen. There was a mood in the air.

Deer season was getting closer. The guys seem to come in, have coffee, listen and not want to talk too much. They are anxious to hear how many deer others are seeing and is there a new bait-food someone is using?

Don mentioned that he must have fed 2 ton of corn to the deer on his land so far this year. He has these 7 day feeders that trip off automatically at a set time on timers. John overhearing this told him that you need more than corn, at least two different baits, sugar beets, carrots, or apples. Why pass up a big buck because you only have corn out and your neighboring camp has more of a variety?

Joe LeBush just came in, sat down, and heard the last comment. Joe smiled and said, "You guys sure spend a lot of money on unnecessary deer bait. Did you ever go to a trout hatchery and watch them feed those little pellets to the fish? They throw a handful out on the water and the fish make the water boil by trying to get the most of them. I saw a visitor there throw a handful of that pea gravel on the water. The fish were used to the pellets being thrown that way and swallowed that fine gravel up too."

One year, I fed shelled corn to the deer by my blind. I ran out of corn but I remembered those trout rising and being fooled by that gravel. Pea gravel is just about the size of a piece of corn. I had a pile of pea gravel at camp so I took a pail full and poured some yellow paint on it, stirred it up and let it dry. The next day, I threw that around by the bait pile.

Now, those deer were either hungry or very competitive. Before daylight, I could hear them crunching on that gravel figuring it was corn. It was so cold out that they probably thought it was frozen corn. The noise they made helped to locate them in the dark. You could even count how many were out there by their crunching sounds." Joe had a twinkle in his eyes as he was telling that "helpful" story and a dead-pan serious face.

Some of the "tourist hunters" were leaning over from another table as close as they could. They then put their heads together, paid their bill, and headed out the door. Joe looked at them and said, "I'll bet they are heading straight for a gravel pit."

After a good laugh, Joe milking this story along, said, "You know the DNR is having problems aging the deer shot near my place. Their (deer) teeth are getting all ground down from eating that gravel. The DNR claims that they are twice as old as they really are because that's how they determine how old a deer is, by the wear on their teeth."

Dick said, "Did Sam tell you about that bear eating out of his bird feeders by his house? Well, here's what he told me. He was cutting grass on his riding mower when he discovered bear droppings on his lawn by his bird feeders. Sam wanted to see that bear so he bought one of those cameras that you set up by your deer post that trips and takes a picture at any time when an animal walks near it. Sam set it up, finished cutting his grass and the next day he saw that all 12 pictures were used up. He took the film in to be developed. When he got it back, the pictures showed him cutting the grass from 12 different angles."

Dick smiled, "Don't ever follow Sam in the woods. He gets lost a lot too." Don offered, "I found a place that grows A LOT of corn. They sell it for $4.00 a hundred but they don't bag it. No cost of bags for them and no extra labor. You tell them how many 100 pounds you want and they put that grain shoot into the back of our pickup and blast it in there. They weigh your truck before and after so they charge you for the difference. If you go there, be sure to duct tape your tailgate of the truck so you don't lose all your corn on the road."

I thought all this advice was just on baiting and gathering bait. Just think what tomorrow might bring? Good luck hunting. Remember if you run short of bait, try the gravel trick.

Gone Huntin

A couple of New Jersey hunters are out in the woods when one of them falls to the ground. He doesn't seem to be breathing, his eyes are rolled back in his head. The other guy whips out his cell phone and calls the emergency services. He gasps to the operator: "My friend is dead! What can I do?" The operator, in a calm soothing voice says: "Just take it easy. I can help. First, let's make sure he's dead." There is a silence, then a shot is heard. The guy's voice comes back on the line. He says: "OK, now what?"

Chapter 11

They Lived Off of the Land

Andy and Jim, they were two pioneers from a lost generation. Hard to explain them any other way. They lived in a real log cabin built by their Grandfather many years ago. It had a slight "list" to it where it was noticeably tipping in that direction.

The U.P. still has many of the hardy souls, just that they are in such remote places that the average person never sees them. They made no attempt to fix that cabin. I suppose that they lived with it every day so they didn't quite pay any attention to it. Two bare light bulbs hanging down inside the cabin appeared to be the only sign of modernization since this place was built, probably more than 150 years ago.

You didn't need any lights turned on to know if Andy was in the cabin after dark. He had a distinct smell to him like decayed forest leaves. A bear would have been happy to roll around on him. (Bears love renascent meat or garbage to roll in).

His brother, Jim, was a little neater but was handicapped. Andy received a small, monthly check for taking care of him. Jim told a friend that he was going to go see if they'd pay him something to take care of Andy as Andy never did anything special for Jim anyway.

This was definitely not a place where Martha Stewart would shine or talk about, "Her beautiful programs for home improvement."

They had a huge, old, wood or coal burning heater in the center of the cabin for heat. It would sizzle all day and night from the "green" wood being burned. The boys felt that "green" wood lasted longer. They did get a few loads of free coal delivered to their door through some social service agency. They called that their "night heat" and saved it for winter nights.

When you'd go into their cabin to visit them (an adventure itself), if it was winter, they'd always look half asleep. Their eyes would be half shut and it appeared like they wiggled their noses slightly, like a bear coming out of hibernation. Or, it could have been from the smoke inside the cabin. It seemed impossible not to have smoke from burning all that green wood.

They loved those surplus food commodities that they qualified for. Andy would go and pick them up with their very old pickup truck. They'd lay out those commodities on their kitchen table (it was their only table). Their eyes would sparkle when they got potatoes, raisins, apples, and sugar. The main ingredients from making homemade "shine" as they called it. They thought that those "town people" were pretty good to provide them with this. "Starves off a cold in the cold weather" Andy explained. "Starves off a cold even in the warm weather." laughed Jim.

They of course hunted some to supplement their "commodity" diet. Andy would drive his old truck into a woods road, turn it so he could shoot across a deer trail out of his truck window. This was rainproof and a comfortable deer blind for him. He could sleep when he wanted to and hunt when he wanted to.

I was visiting there one day when we heard a woodchuck burrowing under the cabin. You couldn't tell if it was trying to get out or in. Andy went outside and shot it. That night, Jim said, "What are we going to have for supper?" Andy told him, "Woodchuck." Jim let it be known that he didn't like woodchuck and asked Andy, "What am I going to eat?" Andy told him, "Whatever you fix for yourself." Jim thought for a while and said, "Think I'll have some of that woodchuck."

Andy would supplement his meager income by pulling out anyone's deer from the woods for $3.00 or $5.00, whatever he could get. The neighboring camps knew this and would go and get him for the long, harder pulls.

I asked Jim if Andy ever worked anywhere. He laughed and said, "He went into the city and signed up for work at a paper mill. They paid him to stand around and watch what to do. Then on the 4th day when he was to work on his own he never showed up. He stayed home. They had to pay him for the 3 days that he watched the others work though."

The social workers that called on them were extremely happy with them. They'd sign them up for the maximum of whatever they had to give. They truly loved this stop. It was a long way out in the county. They collected mileage reimbursement to come and go there. They took pictures of the living conditions and told them not to be in a hurry to change anything. These kinds of pictures justified many people's salaries. They even had to tell them not to smile on the pictures. They didn't want them to appear THAT happy.

One time, when I visited, a social worker had brought two psychologists out there with him. They wanted to do research and experiments with the two men. They had Andy jump on one foot for a few minutes, walk on a low balance beam for 10-20 minutes. This was a piece of cake for Andy who walked on logs in the woods. They wanted Andy to jump to music but there was no place to plug in their recorder.

I asked Andy later why they did this with him. "Seems to pleasure them." he said. "Then they seem to send us more surplus food. "We told them that more apples, raisins, sugar, and potatoes makes us healthier." They promised to send out more. Jim was licking his lips when they said that.

One of the psychologists said, "Notice that Jim there has a twitch in his head and neck. That's a definite sign of someone who cannot work steady." Andy heard that. He thought that he too could convince them that he shouldn't work steady either. Andy started to twitch his shoulders so that his elbows left the tabletop by about four inches. He'd then shake both hands at the same time.

The second psychologist was watching him intently. He leaned over and told the first one, "Watch that one called Andy. I do believe that he's trying to FLY!" Andy would rise off of his chair about a foot with each twitch, just for good measure.

"Maybe it's some of the surplus commodities that give them the extra strength to survive here." Andy said, "Be

48

sure to bring us more of the lighter fluid again next time."
They don't even smoke but they want lighter fluid. Very
curious...must be something creative...I wonder what
they use it for?" (Andy would add it to his batch of
shine. Drinking too much of that could cause you to
"twitch.")

Once they gave us a huge box of powdered milk.
"What's the milk for?" asked Andy. Jim had never seen
anything like that either. "I thought milk came from
cows not from powder in a box." said Jim.

On the way out one social worker asked another. "Do
you think they are Democrats or Republicans?" "I don't
think they know either Party. Notice how happy and
content they seem."

Chapter 12

Action At Carl's Camp

Three of us that normally go fishing in Canada once a year stayed overnight at Carl's camp last Thursday and Friday. We were really looking forward to this. It's located outside of Amberg, WI down a county road about 15 miles then into his road about another 3 miles. The road is windy so you never know that you may see around the next corner. Turkey, deer, and even bear make regular tracks across that road.

The cabin is located on a small lake. All the land around it belonged to Carl and his wife. His dad was a professional logger and somehow acquired this 660 acres that includes a beautiful lake. Ducks, geese, nest on it. Bluegills are starting to bite. There are a lot of other types of fish in there too.

We got there in three different cars as are all good friends but live in different directions. Two pickup trucks and Dave's sports car. I looked at that sports car and thought, it's true. Older boys do have bigger toys.

It was raining when we left home and still raining just as hard when we got there, two hours later. Carl had a wood fire going in the camp. Just enough to keep the dampness out. The camp is furnished so all we had to bring was our shaving gear and a change of clothes. I noticed some of us didn't bring a change of clothes. Carl handles everything else. The refrigerator was full of beverages and makings for a huge spaghetti dinner on Friday. Homemade sausage from Vieu's store in Escanaba (if you ever get a chance to buy homemade sausage from Vieu's, drive out of your way to do it, It's unusually good!) garlic bread, Asiago grating cheese to top off the plate of spaghetti and sausage. When that is simmering you feel kind of special to be invited to this party.

The location is beautiful. Out of the front window you can see most of the lake and the last bend in the road. This peaceful setting is as good as taking three blood pressure pills for those of us who had "high pressure" jobs all of our working lives. The rain was still pouring down. we agreed that the rain seems to get animals moving around. We saw a lot of wild turkey and deer out in the rain on the way into camp. The camp's outhouse was the normal distance behind the camp. Harvey went to use the "facilities" and came back like he saw a ghost! "We got a really big bear by the outhouse, guys!" Harvey shouted. He explained that he was just coming out of the outhouse and that bear was only about 30 feet from him. He said it stomped down hard on its front feet and "Woofed, Woofed" at him like it was daring him to run.

He backed into the camp as quickly as he could. The cabin has an all-metal door that seems to take two hands and a foot to open if it's shut tightly. We shut it TIGHTLY. We turned out the lights and watched and listened for the bear. Nothing but more pouring rain.

That nice rain sound on the roof was relaxing and we decided to call it a night. Bedtime. The wind was coming on stronger. The light items on the long, open, porch were starting to blow off, lawn chairs, cans, and such. We had a good, solid roof. There seems to be nothing more relaxing than hearing pelting rain on a thin roof. This night had all the makings of a deep sleep.

Suddenly, that metal door started making noises like someone was working hard to get in. It started to rock in and out. Then, we heard, "Woof, Woof, Woof." Even with the heavy rain, we knew bear sound. Dave braced a chair under the door knob and Harvey pounded on two kettles to scare it off. It worked. The bear forgot about the door and started licking the grease off of the Weber grill.

No one planned to go outside to relieve themselves after this. The guys suddenly became very creative. One cut a round hole in an empty gallon milk jug, another found an empty three pound coffee can. I still don't know what Dave used. He had the only flashlight so he had "better picking".

The bear left the porch as quietly as he came. Heavy rain continued all night as we slept. The next day, we drove into Amberg for breakfast. It was pouring again and the restaurant was filled with people reluctant to leave.

It's always interesting to go there, mostly local loggers who all sit at one long table. Wide suspenders seemed to be part of the required wear. They all had them, different colors and all about 3" wide. Carl, our camp owner, and also a local, had wide suspenders too. Thin guys had them as well as those with the unlimited bellies.

They all knew Carl and greeted him in loud shouts as we came in. Carl mentioned about the bear around his camp. Norris, one of the locals, well-respected loggers, put his thumb behind one suspender, leaned back on his chair and said, "This week, Monday, there were two bear cubs up in a tree that I wanted to cut down. They made no move to come down, so I started that old Homelite up and proceeded to cut it down. Then I saw a big bear running out of nowhere. It tried to get after me.

Now, you boys know that old chainsaw that I use has power and I had it sharp. I put the saw on full power as that bear took a swipe at me with his paw. I'm here to tell you, I swing that roaring saw at his arm. Believe this or not, guys, but we now have a three legged bear running these woods with two cubs. I think it will have more respect now, when it hears someone with a chainsaw."

The other loggers counted nine other bears that they saw in total roaming the area where they are cutting. They said that the berry pickers and tent campers will probably encounter more bear this year as they don't normally see that many in such a small area.

They all agreed that they'd watch for the 3-legged bear. Then the bear stories got started. "Remember Vic and his wife sleeping in that tent camper in Canada and the bear bouncing it up and down?" A lot of laughter and suspender snapping followed. Made you wish you had a pair of those 3" wide suspenders……..

Chapter 13

A Bare Bones Deer Season

I won't say that I was poor. Anyone going to college isn't thought of as poor but I was going through there on a shoe string. My wife and I were just making it. She was working as a Licensed Practical Nurse at the hospital so we were getting a small check monthly. That paid the rent, gas, and meals. We did a lot of walking and not much driving. There were times when we talked about taking turns eating every other meal.

A Marquette, Michigan climate can be unforgiving to the meek and lazy. We were neither. We found the day old bakery outlet (although, I believe a lot of that stuff was a week or two weeks old). We followed the store sales. One night, there was an ad in the Marquette Mining Journal for 3 lbs of hamburger for $1.00 in Ispheming. That was a ride of about 15 miles away. We drove there for this deal using our limited gas. The next day, Barb fried up some beautiful hamburgers that she made. They were about 5-6 inches in diameter when she put them in the frying pan. You could visibly SEE them shrink up before your eyes as the fat content fried out of them. They later looked like meatballs floating in grease.

We never sought out any welfare or charity. We were determined to do it on our own. The deer season was coming up and we were saving enough for the necessities like gas to get to the camp. Deer season this year meant meat on the table. We were renting an upstairs flat that had a long back porch but no stairs going down outside, a perfect place to freeze meat. In a Marquette winter, anyplace outside was a perfect place to freeze anything. One didn't stand still outside in the winter. If you didn't keep walking, you may not start walking again.

I missed church the first weekend of deer season. For us, that was serious business. During the week, I went to church, into the confessional and told the priest that I missed Sunday church as I went deer hunting. After some silence, he said, "You should have come here first and I could have given you absolution excusing you." That sounded good to a young hunter. I was out of the confessional and half way out of the church when I stopped dead in my tracks. I turned around and went back in there. I told the good priest that I planned on missing again next Sunday to go hunting. Could he give me some absolution for that?

There was a longer silence. Then, he finally said, "Go ahead." That was the only time that I asked for that except when I was best man for one of my Lutheran friend's wedding. That priest said, "Sure, go ahead. We don't count that as a sin anymore." Now, I figured that I had next to God's blessing to go deer hunting. How could I miss?

I had enough of everything gathered for the season except bullets. There were two .30/30 shells left in my box from previous years. That would have to do. No shooting at a target to check the sight alignment. Two shells could do it if I got a good shot. These were the days of the big "deer drives". Camps would come together and about

10-12 hunters would line up a distance apart to walk through 20- 40 acres while more hunters waited on the other end to shoot whatever bucks came running out.

We gathered at Chet's house and barn yard located out in Mid Menominee County. It was so wild near Chet's that deer or bear could be expected to walk between the house and his long-vacated barn. The crowd was steadily getting larger as we all waited for Chet to come out of the house and get the drives started. He was the unchallenged "Drive Boss". He knew the drives, where to post the "standers" and what direction the drivers should move through, considering the wind, and other elements. He knew where the deer should be laying or feeding. He also had a very high success rate in all of these factors. One guy told me, "Chet's been eating venison for so many years that he thinks like a deer." There were now about 8-10 cars and pickup trucks parted in the yard. Everyone had some type of different high powered rifle. I saw some old military rifles that I never knew existed. Chet finally stepped out of the house and said, "Fellas, whoever can shoot good enough, use your rifles and kill me two chickens for supper will you?" Those chickens were walking all around the yard at a slight distance from the hunters. Most everyone smiled and loaded up their rifles. All of a sudden, it sounded like a war had started. .30/30's, .30/06's, semi-automatics from army surplus and shotguns all seemed to go off at once. It was like a fever took over. They kept shooting and reloading. Chickens were flying up in the air for 10-20 feet before they landed. Chicken feathers were drifting loosely in the wind but no dead chickens.

Chet realized that no one could shoot that fast and save even PART of a chicken for him to eat. He quickly shouted, "I mean shoot them in the head not in the body. If you shoot it in the body, you bought it." All the shooting stopped and no dead chickens.

We started out walking from Chet's to the first deer drive. I looked behind and it reminded me of my Army days with a long column of soldiers winding along a trail through the woods. Chet lined up the "shooters" in one column and the "drivers" in another. The shooters went with him to be placed in shooting positions as the column advanced. "Watch out for those Peterson brothers," someone whispered. "They run ahead into the drive trying to get the shot before the deer can run out to the shooters."

Sure enough, when the drive started, the Peterson brothers almost ran into it to get ahead of everyone else, a dangerous place to be if another driver saw a buck. For all their sneaky effort, I never saw them have the opportunity to get a shot. The rest of this hunting group seemed to be good sportsmen and followed all the rules. We came upon a permanent blind built on state land by a landowner who didn't hunt his own 40 but would on the state land bordering it. This group knew that and also knew that he would not allow anyone else to even walk across his land.

Approaching his vacant blind, each one of the column of shooters took one piece each of his blind and continued walking away with it. When the last one in the column got his piece, there was no evidence that a blind ever existed there. They carried those evergreen boughs and boards a good 5 acres away.

The next drive was 40 acres long and it was my turn to be a shooter. Chet was dropping off shooters along the way by good trails to watch when the drive came through. He'd motion with his arms about where to watch and then silently move the remaining column along. No one smoked or talked when you were in Chet's shooting column.

I was the second to last to be placed and Chet, of course, was last. I could hear Chet as he was walking away crushing dried leaves as he walked. It was impossible NOT to make some noise in those 4 inch deep leaves. Finally, I heard Chet stop. I suppose, at his selected post. He no more than stopped when I heard a deer running from his direction over toward me. We were some ridges apart so there was no danger of shooting each other. That deer broke out of the smaller hardwoods and ran within 30 feet of me. It was a nice, high-pronged buck! Chet sure knew his deer trails. I took one shot at its front shoulder and that deer did a perfect summersault about 20 feet from me. It never moved after that. A nice eight-point buck. I levered my second and last shell into the chamber as I heard more crashing in the brush in front of me. Within 2-3 minutes, the Peterson brothers appeared to come out of the swamp where the drive was to take place. They reminded me of seeing two otter as their heads appeared above the low brush looking all around.

Chet waited until the drive was finished, then came over to check what I shot. He sized up the Peterson brothers on the scene well before everyone else and said, "You boys can drag it out." They didn't appear to be to happy dragging out someone else's deer but they knew that you didn't fool with Chet's authority if you wanted to hunt with this group again. After they were a ways ahead,

Chet shook his head, looked at me and said, "You can't pick your relatives." I had a nice buck, one shell to spare, meat for most of the winter, and a wonderful hunt.

Chapter 14

Bear on the Prowl

This happened to a friend of mine in Menominee County, two weeks ago. Monica was going back home after finishing a day's work in Menominee. It was later in the evening when she turned into her country yard as she had worked overtime. It was 8:30 p.m. She knew the time because it was so dark, she was curious and checked her watch.

It probably was clouding up to rain, she thought as there were no stars, the moon was covered over, and it was just plain DARK......

Still nothing to be afraid of......U.P. women are hearty people. They are used to unusual situations and dark nights. Most of the Coop electricity in the county goes off periodically and leaves people in the dark quite often. It becomes a way of life.

Now, I'll try to tell you this story the way she explained it to me. If this doesn't raise the hair on your neck or make you hesitate a little before walking out into the dark, especially if your way out in the country, you are a mighty brave person.

She was home for about a ½ hour and then was due at a friend's house, some 10 miles away. She shut off the

house lights and walked to her car in the very dark yard.
Monica's story: I just felt my way down the porch steps,
tapping each step to find the concrete sidewalk. Finally, I
reached the sidewalk. It's so dark now that I can't see
my car. The car is a Mazda convertible.

Feeling my way to the car, I got the door open and sat on
something that I knew wasn't supposed to be there. I got
out my little flashlight, you know, the kind that fits into
your pocket or purse and never seems to work? I turned
it on, and shined it onto the passenger side. I
immediately noticed that my purse was missing! When I
saw that it was gone. I also noticed some light above my
head. Someone cut or slashed open my convertible car
top! SOMEONE ROBBED ME!!

Worse yet, someone must be out there in the dark yard. I
was all alone. No one else was home. My hands began
to shake. My knees were shaking uncontrollably. I
slowly reached for the door handle, opened the door and
started back toward the house. I fell on one knee, got up
shaking, feeling that SOMEONE WAS OUT THERE!! I
was only in the house previously for ½ hour when this
had to happen.

Reaching the house door, I couldn't get the key into the
lock as I was shaking so badly. Finally I got into the
house and called 911. They told me to lock the doors,
take out a weapon if I had one and stay put. They had a
squad car from the Michigan State Police Post in
Stephenson on the way.

Then I called Don (where I was going) and he said he'd
be right out. Don is a retired Michigan State Trooper and
about the best friend you'd want in a case like this. All

this time, its tombstone quiet out. Dark, and seems to be getting darker if that was possible. I've got the doors locked and I am listening out of a half opened window.

I can hear someone or something kicking in the gravel as they are walking in the yard!!!......Oh man, here I am alone and thinking someone could be stalking me! Then I see Don's headlights coming up the driveway. I can tell by the sound of his jeep. I quickly opened the door and walked out into his headlights. I tell him that someone stole my purse out of the car parked in the yard.

He said, "Get a bigger flashlight." I went into the garage and got the big flashlight. There's no way that I would have went near that garage it I was still there alone. He's got something in his hand but I couldn't make it out in the blackness. You have to live in the country to really understand this blackness. No street light reflection, other car headlights, no nothing for light. Knowing Don, I relaxed some, figuring that he's got his service revolver. I'm still uptight because someone has the advantage of knowing where we are but we don't know where he is.

Don looks around the car, shines the light around the yard and then looks at the car closer. BEAR TRACKS ARE ON AND AROUND THE CAR! He quickly shines the light again around the yard close, then farther away. He tells me to go in and call 911 again to tell them it isn't a robbery and not to send anyone out. I hear the dispatch tell the officer you don't have to go out, it was a bear. But then the officer says, "No, I want to see this. I have never seen anything like this before. So the officer came out. He, Don and I looked around the car and there were bear tracks all over the car and the ground. The tracks led out of the driveway.

The officer took pictures and so did I . Mine were a little shaky though. Holy Wah! Was I ever scared! No one can realize how frightened a person can get unless they are all alone somewhere and you hear sounds and know someone or something is watching you.

Since then we installed motion lights to cover the yard and the house. I was really relieved that it wasn't a stranger out here in that dark. This again all happened in the ½ hour that I was in the house. Just think how close those bear were to me in the dark as I walked back to my car.

I had one of those scent things hanging from the rearview mirror. It had a sweet, berry smell. The men concluded that the bear must have scented that and thought that there was food inside. I probably scared it off when I was locking the house up and walking back to the car in that total darkness. The bear tracks looked like a female with at least one cub from the mud prints in and on the car.

Monica said, "After the fact, everyone had some type of advice to give me. Don't walk around in the dark; install dusk to dawn lights, afraid of a bear? The wolves are something else to watch out for."

Don said, "After a change of underwear, she will need a new car roof, and everything should be fine." Monica looked back at him out of the corner of her eyes like, I'm grateful for all of the help but you had to experience something like that alone, to full understand how it feels......

Chapter 15

Spearing Northern On Charlie's Pond

Growing up in Menominee County years ago, well, there wasn't really that much to do for recreation other than following nature.

You had to be creative, use your imagination more, and hope you survived. It seemed that we'd chase any animal that moved; squirrels, rabbits, porcupines ......just anything.

These were the days when the state distributed chocolate covered goiter pills to be passed out in school. There was a limited iodine salt supply at that time and one of these pills each was suppose to prevent a goiter. We kids never had much chocolate candy in those days. Whatever kid was passing them out would give a big handful to their special friends.

All we realized was that chocolate tasted pretty good. I think we took enough to last two lifetimes. I never did notice any of my friends in adult life with a goiter. We lived through a lot of good meaningful experiences.

The following is a story about my two friends, Joseph and Brian. In the spring, the ice would melt off of the Menominee River gradually, then, one particular day, it was like someone opened a flood gate downriver. The ice would break up, make some of the loudest crashing noises, and move quickly downstream. There was no stopping it. Whoa to anything that was in its way. Old wooden boats not pulled completely up on the bank earlier, boat docks, anything in its way went downstream.

The small backwater ponds along the river would also become ice-free at the same time. It seemed that the main river's ice literally sucked the ice right out of these ponds and pulled it along with. As soon as that surface ice cleared itself away, the backwater ponds and some streams became ideal spawning areas for northern pike.

The northern would swim upstream into flooded farm fields and creeks. The spawning would begin quickly in these shallow water areas. Neighborhood men would take up positions around this one field pond with spears, hay forks, and shotguns, to get a few northern as they swam by or would stop along the grassy shore.

We kids had no idea if this was legal or illegal. We only knew that they looked like they sure were having fun. It was on Charlie's private land and a long way from any public road. Some had hip boots on, and some stood on high rocks or stumps. We knew one thing, a spring northern did taste good.

Joseph, our best backwoods partner and creative thinker said, "Those men only try to catch those fish on the weekends because of their work. We could go there and get some fish DURING the week. There wouldn't be any adults there to move us away. Brian and I would have free sailing. Next week Tuesday, school is closed for teachers inservice, whatever that means."

"Brian, why don't you 'borrow' your Dad's spear, and I'll 'borrow' my Dad's shotgun. We can get them back before they miss them."

Joseph was always good at coming up with a plan. They'd always be so excited toward starting the new one that they had a tendency to forget that the old ones never really came off without some type of problem.

On Tuesday, they were riding their bikes out towards "Charlie's Pond". Joseph had the spear tied to his bike frame just under the seat and up past the front wheel sprocket. His leg was over it as he rode so it wasn't noticeable. Brian had the shotgun across the handle bars in a gun case. No one paid any attention to it. This was long before people worried about terrorist or Iraqi spies. Joseph could have passed for either of them. He didn't wash up to often and when he did, it was only where he thought it was necessary.

After a 6 mile ride, they arrived and were all excited to start, Joseph, always the generous one, said, "Brian, when you stun one with the shotgun, I'll run out quickly and bring it in." Brian always knew there were reasons why he liked him for a hunting and fishing partner. "Of course, he said, "I get first pick of any fish we get for jumping in that cold water." It still sounded like a good deal to Brian.

They "fished" for about an hour and Joseph got one medium sized northern and missed two more. Brian saw ripples being made close to the shore. Soon, a good sized northern tail came above the water. That fish was about 3 feet long. He shot under it to stun it. Joseph, true to his word, came running over but by the time he got there, the fish came to again, and swam away.

He said, "Shoot right at them next time and see what happens." Next time was about ½ hour away. Another northern swam by near the shore. It swam about 4 feet away from the end of the gun barrel. Brian shot, water splashed up all over him. The fish was flopping around on the waters surface. Joseph charged in there like he was used to it.

He held that fish against his chest and walked back to the shore. It was wiggling and fighting to get free all of the way in. By now, Joseph was all wet and cold. He said, "I'm too cold to run into the water anymore today. Let's quit for now." "OK," agreed Brian. He had that retrieving down pat and Brian didn't want to take anything away from him.

He wondered what Joseph's parents would say when he came home so wet. "Don't worry." Joseph said. "They're always happy when I bring home something to eat." This was an annual spring happening in the creeks and backwaters in Menominee years ago...............

Chapter 16

Trapper Pete and the Grass Widow

Trapper Pete was, of course, a trapper by occupation. He lived in a comfortable cabin as he called it. He had running water inside, a good cement floor, and it was insulated. The limited experience he had with girls was talking briefly with the check-out girl at the local grocery store. He was the only person that I knew that had a huge St. Bernard dog. That dog was about waist high standing on all fours if he walked near you. It was huge. Pete would have it pull his homemade trapping supply sled when he'd make his rounds.

He could also stand on the back runners of the sled. That dog, he called him Ralph, was so strong that he wouldn't notice the extra weight. My friend, Carl, and I were single at this time so we'd visit Pete often. He was usually skinning out some hides and he'd tell the most interesting stories. He would say, "The only thing missing in my life is a woman to share things with. It gets pretty lonely sometime here with only Ralph."
Pete would say that so often that we thought we'd take it upon ourselves to find the "right girl" for him. We lived in town and knew more people. The people living near Pete seemed to take him for granted. It never crossed any girl's mind out there to be interested in him. We thought about it for awhile and counted up Pete's assets. He owned a cabin and land, owned two pickup trucks, one to

drive on roads and the other one looked like it never drove on a road but only through the woods.

There weren't many girls interested in a guy like Pete. We started to make a possible list and we kept crossing them off for one reason or another. We did finish with one name. It was Miss Lilly Albright, a school teacher that lived alone and seemed about Pete's age. (We figured that he was somewhere around 50.) Everyone that talked about her called her a Grass Widow. We weren't sure what that meant but figured it (grass) was something close to nature so that would fit in with Pete.

She'd always dress just proper and didn't seem to have a lot of company ever at her house. We noticed that on some Sunday afternoons, the local Reverend would visit and have tea or coffee with her. (She was known as a good donator to the church.) That seemed to be the extent of her social life from what we could see.

All of that quiet was about to change. We were going to figure out how to fix Pete and her up together. Now, Pete seemed to love that big St. Bernard dog of his. That dog was big all over. He had a head almost as big as a horse. Its eyes were full-size, like a person's. It forever had its tongue hanging out and enjoyed licking anyone that came near it. It drooled a bit from its mouth which added to a very mushy lick if he licked your face.

That and being extra big, he was a little oxy around furniture in a house. Carl and I started to form a plan. We'd convince Pete that the Widow Albrecht was looking for a man, an outdoors man. Then we'd help him to be more presentable and coach him a bit on boy-girl stuff. Carl had an older sister and we watched her and her boyfriend operate when they though no one was watching them.

We talked over what seemed to work and what didn't in their courting. The list was short but we felt we had some positive pointers for Pete. After all, The Grass Widow wasn't expecting him to come over. We felt that was a plus. Then we coached him on how to sound proper and presentable to this fine lady.

Pete was skeptical but felt that he had nothing to lose. The next Saturday, she was home relaxing from a week of tensions at school. Pete pulled up to her house with his newer truck and with Ralph sitting beside him. Pete knocked on the door, introduced himself and said he was interested in being a speaker on wildlife in her class. She smiled and invited him in. All teachers seem to be a push-over for something free, especially for a speaker that didn't cost anything. She taught Biology and was interested in any type of wildlife. Pete had a natural "in."

It wasn't long and they were enjoying coffee and cake together. One thing led to another and they were soon in the front room laughing like teenagers. Now that Grass Widow was showing signs of being interested in Pete, as a man. She had a hungry look in her eyes. Pete wanted to show her how strong his hands were so he pinned her down on the sofa. Suddenly, they kissed, Pete thought, this is better than petting his St. Bernard, Ralph. She had her eyes closed as Pete kissed her again and again.

Ralph, his faithful companion, sensed a happening. St. Bernard's are smart dogs. It opened the truck door and strolled over to the back door of the house. It slobbered some, but opened the house door with its mouth. Then, it saw Pete kissing the Grass Widow who now had her eyes shut. It waltzed over along side of Pete and started to lick the Grass Widow's face. Its tongue was about a foot long and 6 inches wide. A few slobbering licks and she started to choke.

She opened her eyes and had a hard time believing what she saw. She screamed (as we told Pete later, screams of passion) tried to get up but Pete still had her pinned to the sofa. She raised her legs and somehow got Pete's neck in a "leg lock." He told us later, that she had the strength of an ox, (Carl and I had heard somewhere before that fear will do that to you.) She threw Pete off the couch like wrestler's do on TV. The dog licked her on the face again. She sprang up and ran around the room to get away. It was a very big and spacious room. Ralph, the dog, would follow anything that ran. He was strolling behind her. She jumped over an easy chair. Ralph jumped too but being so big and clumsy, he tipped over that big chair. She then made a bee-line into the bathroom and slammed the door shut.

Pete got up, rubbed his neck, and said, "Ralph sure likes you. He doesn't normally warm up to a stranger that fast." He could hear her gasping for air in there. Pete never did like small rooms. Not enough oxygen he'd always say. She gasped, "What is THAT thing and where did it come from?" "That is my dog, Ralph." Not many people ever asked where it came from so Pete took that as a compliment. He told her, "I traded an old saw rig for him a few years ago. Are you going to come out of there?"

She said, "First, get that big dog out of the house." Pete convinced her that Ralph would mind good and lay in the

71

kitchen. Her kitchen had a cabinet counter so that she could stand on one side and Pete and the dog were on the other side. She looked slowly over the counter, skeptical of that huge dog and now more skeptical at Pete.

Pete said, "Do you have any meat that you can give Ralph? He'll settle down more if he has meat." She opened the refrigerator and took out a plastic wrapped package of cold meat. The Grass Widow had on a dress and an apron tied in front of it. As she had the refrigerator open, somehow, Ralph walked over and sat down in front of her to look into the refrigerator. The dog's head and body was between her apron and her dress. Its tail was sticking way out between her legs wagging back and forth on the floor behind like a giant windshield wiper. She looked behind her and saw that tail swishing back and forth between her legs. At first glance, it looked like that tail belonged to her! Ralph somehow, looked up and "cold nosed" her under her dress. She screamed again and threw the plastic coated meat package behind her. Ralph, the oversized St. Bernard, stood up and turned around to get the meat. She was now literally riding Ralph like a small horse.

She grabbed the cabinet counter, jumped off, and stared at Ralph who was eating the meat and plastic all as one. There was now a puddle of drool a good yard wide on the floor where he was eating. That kitchen was immaculately clean otherwise.

Pete finally got Ralph to go outside. She said, "Go see what your dog is doing in the yard." Pete told us that he went outside and she slammed the door and locked it. He could hear her as she worked 3or 4 different locks on the door.

Pete said, "I hollered in to her that I'd still come to her class, it sounded like she said, "When Hell freezes over" and "When pigs fly." We convinced him that the screams were all signs of "emotional love." But, we told him that he best stay away from there for awhile. Grass Widows can be unpredictable.....................

Chapter 17

Game Warden Caught in Own Bear Trap

Believe it or not, DNR personnel are human too. We hear so many negative stories about incidence's with game wardens that it's easy to believe that they are ALL bad. Some of these stories we've heard about, in most cases, was a lack of common sense judgment by an individual and then it's easy to believe that they are all the same.

Don't get me wrong. We all sweat a little when we see one coming in the woods. You think, "Do I have my license or did I leave it back in the camp? Am I doing ANYTHING wrong?" I guess it's a natural worry as you know their job during hunting season isn't coming to give you a weather report. Finding something wrong is good for them and bad for you.

I've got to tell you about one of my newly acquired friends, Tim. He is a game biologist with the DNR. Two summers ago, I drove into my camp road and planned on staying at camp for a few days. There's nothing like a few days at camp to relax. I settled in and it soon got dark. I should explain that I have a 10 foot by 20 foot screened in porch attached to the front of the camp, a safety zone to keep the mosquitoes out of camp, a cool place to sleep on very hot summer nights. A place where you know you're safe by merely hooking the screen door.

We keep the garbage can out there. Before deer season, we pile three rows of heater wood out there. You can hear whippoorwills at night, maybe an owl hooting, mosquitoes buzzing on the other side of the screen, and a few twigs snapping in the woods as some animal is passing through. It was always so peaceful.

I don't sleep out there anymore! My wife says after I fall asleep, a cannon could go off and I'd still stay sleeping. This one night (I was actually sleeping inside) I woke up and sat up in the bed. Something was bouncing that 30 gallon metal garbage can up and down on the cement floor of the porch. It sounded similar to an army sergeant we had in basic training that would pound a club on the sides of an empty garbage can in our barracks to wake us up.

I took the flashlight and found my way to the front door. This was about 3:00 in the morning. Turning on the porch light, I saw the biggest and blackest bear that I ever want to see up close. There was about 4 inches of moldy corn left in that garbage can from deer season and he was shaking it loose out of that can. I hollered at it and turning quickly, it ran out right through a section of screen like it wasn't even there.

The next day, I checked around the camp carefully. The bear had pulled the screen door off of one hinge to get in. It also scratched its claws onto the electric light pole at the edge of the camp clearing. His scratch marks were about 8-10 feet high and covered about 18 inches up and down. There were splinters hanging out of that pole where he scratched (about 5 inches long) like someone shot that pole many times with a high powered rifle.

I showed the "pole markings" to my brother-in-law who came up the next day. "Now, you have problems," he said. "That bear is marking his territory so other bears stay clear of here." After looking at it longer, he commented, "He sure must be a big one. Those pole scratches are high up on the pole. Look, I can hardly reach that high. I didn't think it was possible for anything to pull splinters like that out of one of those creosol light poles."

I had heard stories that the DNR would come and trap rogue bear and move them somewhere else. That sounded like a good idea so I drove into town and met the personnel at the DNR station. The first person that I met in there was a female secretary. She said, "Whatever you want, I probably don't know much about it as I'm new here." I figured what a line THAT is. I could use that on my job back home when an irate party comes in to complain. Then a real game warden walked through. He looked at me like he would have liked to pounce on me and handcuff me. Or that's how it appeared to me. He didn't smile and didn't seem to blink his eyes when he was staring at me. I had a timber wolf stare at me like that once. I felt lucky that I was in my pickup truck at the time or he would have had me for lunch.

I started thinking, "What am I doing here?" Then, after telling the now "well-covered" and "off-the-hook" secretary my bear problem, she introduced me to Tim, the Game Biologist. He was a likable guy from the start. He smiled, never stared at me, didn't jiggle his handcuffs and really seemed like he was interested in what I had to say.

I told him about my bear problem, where my camp was located, and asked if he could set up one those barrel-type live bear traps that they have mounted on trailers. At first, he said, "That bear is probably long gone by now. He came because he smelled food and probably is miles away by now. You know, it's mating season and he's probably covering a large area. He'd have to do noticeable damage for us to set up a trap for you." I told him that it pulled my screen door off and some siding off of the porch. It also left its "territory marks" high on a pole by the camp. He became more serious and said, "Sounds like you HAVE got a problem all right. Territory marks mean it plans on coming back or is going to stick around." "How long are you going to be at your camp? I can bring a live trap out there tomorrow."

Tim came bouncing in with that bear trap on a trailer the next day. The trailer looked like it was purchased by the State as "lowest bid" or else it had broken springs on one side. The barrel trap seemed to be fighting to stay on the trailer. He immediately set it up and as he was making adjustments and cranking up the guillotine spring-loaded back door, he lectured me that I would have to check the trap each day as a bear would be in danger of dying from heat if left in that barrel for long, etc. etc.

The trap was round like a good-sized 70 gallon barrel. It had a bait trigger inside toward the front. The bait is attached to the trigger bar. When anything pulls on the bait and moves the trigger, the back door slams shut and locks anything inside. Tim cranked up the back door and moved a wedge in place so the door locked open. He then crawled into it with a pound of rancid bacon and proceeded to tie it to the trigger of the trap (same principle as a rabbit box trap except bigger).

As he's talking and tying the bait, he's also pulling somewhat on the trigger that he's tying it to. BANG! Without any warning, the back door slammed shut as he pulled too hard on the bait trigger. All was quiet inside the trap. I think he was checking if his feet were still attached to his legs. Luckily he was completely inside the trap. That door really slammed down!!

Trying to sound matter-of-factly and professionally, he said, "Now you've got to be very careful so this don't happen if you re-bait the trigger. Ah......would you crank up the door so I can get out? It's impossible to get out otherwise." I smiled and said, "This would be some joke for your partners back at the office to know you're locked in a bear trap." Tim looked worried and said, "We're pretty good friends already aren't we? I'm sure you wouldn't tell anyone about this, would you?" I smiled and let him sweat for awhile. "I'll tell you what. When we go back to town, I'll buy coffee for a good understanding that no one hears about this but us." Having a little fun, I said, "Coffee's cheap, Tim." I'll throw in a chicken dinner and a piece of pie if you'll crank that door open right now." I said, "I might have my camera in the car if you want a picture of this." "No pictures!" Tim pleaded.

Cranking that door open was easy and I never saw a more relieved and grateful guy. "On second thought, don't go in there to re-bait. Just throw the new bait in ahead of the trigger." He said. "Good advice. After seeing you so helpless in there, I had no intention in ever going in there." Tim since has transferred to the "Mother House" of the DNR in Lansing, Michigan. It's a step up for him and I'm sure, it opens the door for more opportunities. With his personality, he'll make a very positive

78

improvement in some department there. We never did catch the bear but we had some good laughs and made a new friend.

Chapter 18

A Bear in the Camp!

Last September, our fishing party, of four guys, was driving up to WaWa, Canada for an annual fly-in fishing trip. John, Jerry, Bill and I had made this trip before. One of the highlights of the trips into Canada is seeing a moose or a bear. If you're lucky, one will either run across the road in front of your truck or be seen standing alongside of the road somewhere.

These trips have a lot of humdrum miles to drive. We usually relive some past adventures or do some, "What if" stories for the new trip. What if we get rain for the whole week up there? What if we're bothered by some wild animal by the camp for the week? There are cougar, black bear, and moose around there. All of these animals are possible to see as this is a fly-in trip many miles from your normal "drive in" sportsmen. We fly-in for about an hour over some very rough and roadless terrain.

Landing the pontoon plane onto the lake that we fish and unloading our week's supplies of provisions is our last contact with any other humans for a week. There is only one cabin on the lake. It fits four people nicely.

We did see some very huge bear paw prints in the sand alongside of the lake last year. They were fresh enough that everyone kept looking over their shoulder whenever you left the cabin. Bill was saying, "If a bear ever got into the cabin while we were in it, you could climb up into the open rafters. There's room up there to move around and stay away from it." I thought he sure has those bear on his mind from our stories on the way up.

The cabin has a long table and some "rummage sale chairs" for eating, card playing, or reading. The other end of this room has a kitchen sink, gas refrigerator, gas stove, and some open shelves. Open shelves means some shelves like you have at home in your own kitchen but without any doors on them. For a week's stay, you can just look at those shelves and see what groceries are left, and how many dishes are still clean.

There's a wood heater in the center and an outside door just opposite of it. Two bedrooms make up the rest. There are two double bunks in each room (one on top and one on the bottom). They are made sturdy enough, with 2x4's and one inch lumber. Each bedroom has a door opening without a door facing the main room. All in all, it's plenty of room for four people. There is always some wildlife sign around the cabin, probably not any more than you'd find anywhere else beside that lake, but it's there.

For some reason, bear talk took over the conversation from most of those miles. No one wanted to say it but even going to the outhouse, one would make extra noise with their mouths singing or such, anything to feel a little more secure in bear country. This was not passing through, country for bear. They actually lived here. These were some of the last thoughts that we had when we went to sleep that night.

I should mention, because I have a sinus problem, I have to sleep part of the night sitting up in a chair. My wife is used to this at home, but I guess, this was something new to people that you don't live with everyday. In this camp, I set a chair alongside of that long table sideways. I rested one elbow on the table and on the other side is huge picture window, probably 8 feet square facing the lake. On a moonlit night, a lot of natural light comes into the camp. That is the ONLY light in the camp at night.

The second night was colder. Sitting in that chair to sleep was more of an endurance test than a good sleep. I thought for a while, what did I bring with to off set that cold? I had won a set of either long underwear or a lounging suit from the Duck's Unlimited Banquet this fall. It was fleece lined, had the Duck's Unlimited insignia on it and I had brought it with.

Everyone else seemed to be snoring loudly. Each one was probably dreaming of something different. A trophy fish, seeing a bear or a moose, or are we going to portage to the other lake tomorrow, a lake over the hill always seems to be better than the one you are fishing in. So we all think.

As much as any sportsmen tell their wife's or girlfriend's that they dream about them up there, they don't. They dream of their OWN safety. Well, I quietly got out that nice, fleece-lined, underwear and started to put it on. That was a job in the dark as that long underwear was JET BLACK ITSELF! It was hard to tell if it was inside out or not in the dark.

After a while, I was resting comfortably in a chair, sitting up by that moonlit picture window. Just before I drifted off to sleep, I can remember looking out and seeing the Canadian mist settling above the water, a very peaceful sight. Walden's Pond had nothing over this. Gradually, the mist covered the entire lake and was creeping a bit onto the land.

Then Bill got up intent on going outside to do a nature call. He got as far as the main room, stopped, and shouted, "There, There, THERE'S A BEAR IN THE CAMP!" The door had no lock on it and it was possible that anything could open it. "He kept shouting, "IT'S OVER BY THE TABLE!" I jumped up with a start and tripping on my blankets, fell on all fours. I'm nearsighted and had my glasses back in the second bedroom where I started to sleep.

When he said, "IT'S OVER BY THE TABLE." I ran over near him as I couldn't see in the dark that clearly without my glasses. He ran back into his bedroom and climbed up the ladder into the top bunk. I ran behind him and also climbed up to that bunk. I figured he could see a lot better than I could. He looked behind, and then jumped across into the other top bunk in the room. John was sleeping there. I followed Bill, by the time that I got into that 2nd top bunk, John jumped down to the floor and ran somewhere. Bill then reached the rafters and did a balancing act to get above the main room and out of the bear's reach.

I started into the rafters, a little slower as I couldn't see then as clear as he could. Bill started screaming, "WOO, WOO, WOOH!" trying to scare the bear away. Jerry and John shouted, "We're making a break for the outhouse!" That outhouse was new and very well built. Bill pleaded, "Help me down from here!" He was about 8 feet above the floor. "Jump!" one them hollered. Bill jumped. Thank goodness he didn't break anything as he rolled around on the floor. He was out the door and in that outhouse before they could close the door.

All was quiet in the camp. I listened for what seemed like 10 minutes, that bear must have ran out the door too as I couldn't hear it inside. Climbing back to the floor, I went into the other bedroom and got my glasses and flashlight. No bear in sight so I shut the door.

The fright and running around really warmed me up. I then took off that black, long underwear. Opening the window facing the outhouse, I called out, "Guys, there's no bear in camp now. He must have run out too." I could see a head poke out of the outhouse and look all around. Then, John, the newest guy on the trip stepped out and walked slowly, very slowly, back toward he came. They must have convinced him that he could run faster or promised him the use of the "good motor" on his boat if he went out first.

Then, the others came out close behind him. No one wanted to be last in line. If a cougar would have made one of those high pitched screams like they do at times, I could have had three scared to death fishing partners. Bill lit the two ceiling gas lights and was saying, "You can never be careful enough. I don't know how it got in. I said, "What's that smell? Smells like one of you didn't make it to the outhouse without having an accident." Bears can be tricky business, especially when you're right in bear country.

Chapter 19

A Michigan Family Vacation "Getaway"
Or Was I Crazy?

Tobin, one of my good friends, planned to take his family on a Michigan camping vacation. He remembered how his parents took him when he was a kid and how much he enjoyed it.

Tobin's kids would learn about the Great Outdoors, go swimming, fishing, hiking, and they rented a few videos for backup in case it rained. Tob, as everyone call him, rented a crank up camper trailer with a few luxuries, a refrigerator, big enough to hold pop for the kids and little else. A TV and video player that was also small but it would work. Their source of cooking fire was a small Weber grill. This was a step up from kneeling on the ground with a campfire to cook.

They loaded it up, filled the car with surplus items and were READY! Starting off on Saturday, they had 3 hours to drive to the Shaky Lakes County Park that had swimming, fishing, campsites, and seemed to be one step up from what Tob experienced as a boy camping in a tent.

I should tell you a little about this family. Tob, himself, was an old Yooper from way back. He could enjoy nature and not need ANY luxuries. He grew up from a family of 12. He told me, "To get a pair of socks to wear, you had to wake up before ½ of the others did." His wife had an opinion about everything. The first thing she expressed it on was this camping trip. She was against it before it started.

Then the kids. Mary was all spit and polish. She wasn't used to getting sand between her toes or sharing such a small space as this trailer. After all, a one girl family always has their own room. Then the two boys, Peter and Paul. Peter was declared hyperactive, according to his teacher and the school. The neighbors just said that he was NUTS! Whatever you told him not to do, he would gladly do.

His older brother, Paul, was normal enough, but seeing the camping equipment that his Dad threw together, and the small pace in that camper trailer that they all were to share, he felt that this trip was going to qualify as some type of child or family abuse for a week.

Tob said, "We got a great start on Saturday. The kids were reluctant to sing but I got them started and then they couldn't seem to stop. It was getting like they were working hard at grinding on their parent's nerves."

The little camper trailer turned out to be a mistake. We had to eat the meals outside but we were prepared for that. There was a nice picnic table right by our camper trailer. The only source of a cooking fire was that Weber grill that should have done the job nicely.

We were spreading things out, getting the grill lit and the beds ready for the evening. Then, it started to rain. We all ran inside and waited for it to quit. Tess had the hot dogs and hamburgers all ready to put on the grill as soon as this rain stopped. Only.........it didn't stop. It began to rain so hard that the little camper trailer started to sway back and forth. If you stepped one foot outside of that camper, you would be drenched. It was now shaping up to be an all day and maybe an all night rain.

I looked at the Weber grill smoking. It was going out like someone poured a pail of water on it. The bag of charcoal was outside by the grill and getting just as soaked. So far, the family was holding out well. We've been called names before, like, "The family from Hell" by some of the neighbors.

The rain was pelting off of our canvas roof and I told the boys not to touch the canvas roof because wherever you touch it, it will leak water inside. Crazy Peter had to be the first one to test it (the neighbors called him "Crazy Peter" and we were getting used to it). That water came in just as their Dad told them it would. "Don't touch any more!" Their Dad shouted. Crazy Peter needed something more to keep him busy. The school recommended easing him off of his hyperactive medicine for the summer. The family was starting to feel the results of it. The tent was now dripping steady in four or five places where "someone" touched the canvas.

What's the next normal thing that people do after sitting out a rain, hearing it come down, feeling its effects from the dripping? They had to go to the toilet. The toilet was approximately 75 yards away from their campsite. The kids dashed out into the rain and ran out of sight. It was a heavy rain. The dog ran along with them in the rain. 15 minutes later, they came back, wet as wet could be.

The dog did what dogs do first. It shook all the water off inside the camper. What wasn't already wet was now getting a heavy mist of a shower from the dog. The kid wanted dry clothes. Everyone wanted to eat. We ate raw hot dogs and raw hamburgers.

The neighbors' smoke from their grill was filling up our camper. They had a canvas roof over their fire and also over the tables that they were eating from. Those barbecued hamburgers smelled as good as a nice steak. Then Tess got started. "Why don't WE have a nice roof for OUR table to eat under? Did you really expect all five of us and the dog to stay bunched up in this little trailer?" The storm is now started to flash lightning, heavy thunder, and the rain is coming down in sheets. I'm not sure what you would call it, Depression, Hate, or Revolution is setting in.

A neighbor on the other side of us is beginning to swear at each other. They are loud and probably depressed with the storm. It was not a good environment for the kids. Or hyperactive boy, Crazy Peter, was trying to push the dog out into the rain. The dog was fighting back and hollowing that it didn't want to go.

The other kids were bored because by now, they saw the same videos over and over again. My wife said, "Are you happy now? You have everyone upset." I looked around, everyone except Crazy Peter. He was all smiles. He had done something to someone but for the life of me, I couldn't figure out what it was.

A family getaway? Never do it in a small trailer camper. All the way home, I heard, "Are we almost there yet?" "How much farther?" "I told you this was a poor idea."

"Now you have to go to my mother's house for a week tradeoff like you promise." And, for God's sake, don't tell her the truth of what you think of her cooking like you did on the last visit. She didn't speak to us for a month after that."

The only one truly happy on this getaway, was Crazy Peter. He was smiling from ear to ear as he rolled up the dog's tail in the power windows of the car.

Chapter 20

The Best Christmas Present...........

Our "Sportsmen" were sitting around having coffee at Shank's place this week. Shank is the only one in our group that is not married. He has the only house where we can go to and truly relax. You can sit around the table with your boots on, never mind the snow on them. It melts into nice puddles on the floor. The dog wonders over once in a while and slurps up some of the bigger puddles.

"The wood fire will dry up the rest, guys. Don't worry about it," Shank said. We married guys WERE getting worried when some of that water started to run into the next room. Marriage and a good nagging wife will do that to you.

"This sure is nice and relaxing," explained Bill with a big smile. He was stamping that snow off onto the floor, watching the water run and was really enjoying it, making a little water on the floor and no one to holler at him. This was like, "Man's last cave." Shank passed around a long roll of smoked venison sausage and a butcher knife. Each one cut off a good inch, peeled the casing off, ate it and passed the rest to the next guy. That butcher knife was so long that you had to be careful it didn't cut you on the other side of the table.

Good sausage though. He had a habit of naming his deer when he put them away in his freezers. Notice that I said freezers? Shank filled more than one. "That sausage came from Peter. He's in the chest freezer downstairs." Carl looked skeptical over his shoulder at the doorway going downstairs, and then went back to eating. That salami was about 2 feet long when Shank brought it out, now, it disappeared at the last cutting.

What was the best Christmas present? Bob said, "I got a lot of good things this year. One that I think about is a two-way radio set. They should come in handy when we go to Canada this fall. Truck to truck traveling. We HAD a pair last year. Bill gave me one to use in our boat and he kept one so we could communicate between the boats. The only problem, he kept his in his shirt pocket. When he bent over to get into the boat, PLOP!......It slid out and dropped into the water. We found out quickly, water resistant does not mean waterproof! We were back to hand signals between the boats again.

On the plus side, the directions that came with them say that they are active up to a 6-mile range. I wonder if that counts going through evergreen and hardwood trees from the deer blind to the camp? It says that they are water resistant. That probably means if you have one in camp and one in a watertight deer blind. No direct contact with water.

It has a "vibra alert" for silent paging (if someone from the camp wanted to talk to me). Now, if anyone looked into my deer blind and saw me dozing and my pants pocket vibrating steady...... it would be hard to explain that it was from a two-way radio in my pocket. I've got some unusual guys that I hunt with at times. There are nights when you hesitate closing your eyes after "light out time."

Dave said to watch what you say on that thing from your deer blind. You will have every game warden in a 6-10 mile radius keying in on you.

Barb, my good wife, said, "If I need you at camp to bring in more wood or to do some other chores, I can always call you. Yes, I think buying you those for Christmas was a good idea." Bill and I were in camp when she came up with this very helpful idea. After she walked outside, Bill said, "Remember what happened to my set in Canada? You could always set your receiver in a pail of water back in the deer blind. No one would bother you."

I was thinking, I could use it to call someone to help drag out my deer next year. Years ago, we'd walk in and tell someone to "bring the rope" meaning, I need help dragging in my deer. Now, we just ask someone to "bring the 4-wheeler." That's God's answer to help a hunter in "skidding" out a deer. Tie it behind the 4-wheeler's trailer hitch and the deer will skid perfectly behind the 4-wheeler just like nothing was there.

Maybe those 2-way radios will be OK after all...............

Cedarville..................I drove to Cedarville this weekend for an author's meeting. I discovered a few things from that trip. It is a long ways to Cedarville. Evidently, not many people can find it as there weren't many of us up there. My superior tracking skills and asking at a few gas stations made it no problem for me.

What a beautiful place! It's located on a big lake and seems to be a very friendly little community. I stayed at the Cedarville Inn and ate at Angli Los and also at Pami's. Both had excellent food. Pami's has a Friday Night Fish Fry with fresh fish out of Lake Superior. All you can eat, perch. What a rare treat!

It was 13 below up there Friday night. Outside, it sounded like you were walking on Styrofoam from the cold, dry, frozen snow. I was invited over to the (way north friends) on Friday night for a visit. It was COLD going out of that motel. The door on my pickup truck sounded like it was fighting to stay closed when I finally got it open. The dashboard lights stare back at me, like, "Is this trip really necessary." One gauge wouldn't work, then, finally kept jumping back and forth like a fast pendulum on a clock. I figured out later, that it was for the battery. The battery worked well, just that the gauge didn't in the cold.

A well-insulated house, a fireplace going for extra warmth and a relaxed feeling, and good company, I could hear off in a far direction, a timber wolf howling. I think we'd have been howling too, if we were out in that cold.

My grandson, Cal on his first fishing outing.
If patience counts, He's now hooked for life.

Chapter 21

Cal's First Fish

There are many unforgettable experiences that we all have in life. Watching your son take his first steps, your son cutting grass alongside of you with a toy lawn mower, or sitting in your deer blind with you watching for a deer. These are just a few, for a sportsman.

I had that privilege twice, once with my son and second with my grandson. What seems to make these things special is that I can reflect back when I did the same thing many years ago with my Dad.

My first fish was caught in the backwater pond along the Menominee River. The pond was big enough that some older people had built a log raft and had it tied to the shore on one side of the pond when they weren't using it. There were a lot of rafts around at that time. Building it was easy. A paper mill had huge log piles within 30 feet of that pond. The raw material was right there. We younger kids would "borrow" the raft when the bigger ones weren't around. Poling that raft out farther into the pond and having wild imaginations, we were reliving Huckleberry Finn and Tom Sawyer all over again.

Suddenly, we saw FISH swimming near the far shores. Pan fish and they don't seem to spook too much. The next day, we were back with worms, fish line and hooks.

Cutting a pole was easy, it didn't seem to take any time and we had a few nice pan fish on the raft. There was no water current so poling wasn't a problem. Everything seemed more relaxed at that time.

Now it was my grandson's turn. My cousin, Jerry, has a pontoon boat that makes top-of-the-line luxury fishing. Jerry also grew up fishing from a raft when he wanted to go out on the water. He now has a river flowage right in front of his yard. There are plenty of fish around there. We pulled into his driveway on a Saturday with the main goal of helping my grandson, Cal, catch his first fish. Jerry's neighbor was out in her yard and saw us. She overheard us talking that we were taking little Cal out fishing. "Do you have a life jacket for the little guy?" she asked. We were going to give him an adult sized one. "Wait a minute," she said. She disappeared into the garage and came out with a life jacket that fit Cal perfectly. "My kids used these and I can tell you, they will float him like a cork."

That's one thing about "Yooperland." Most neighbors treat each other like family. (Yooper is derived from "U.P.", initials for the Upper Peninsula of Michigan). Worms were hard to get at this time of the summer (early August) but Jerry managed to save some in his worm bed.

This was 6 year old Cal's first experience on a pontoon boat, probably, any boat. He stepped on and it tipped ever so slightly. He stopped dead in his tracks and looked at us like, "Is this normal?" After about one minute, it seemed like he was well adjusted to the boat's motions.

Jerry fired up the 25 horsepower motor, eased us away from the shore and over to some of his favorite fishing grounds. We anchored and rigged up the poles. Jerry cast out Cal's line and we coached him on watching his bobber, how to pull to hook a fish, and "don't get excited and throw in the pole".

In a matter of minutes the bobber started sliding sideways across the water's surface. Then it started bobbing up and down. "Pull, Cal!" I shouted. He leaned back with his pole like you would hook a walleye. He had it hooked and a pan fish is one of the best fighters for anyone to catch. That pole was flexing like he had on a 5-pounder. We just watched so he didn't get excited and throw the pole in.

He landed it in the boat himself. Now, if you want to truly see a happy boy, the expression on his face was an experience to behold. That pontoon boat may have been a touch of luxury but I guess Jerry and I could see ourselves many years ago doing the same thing from a homemade log raft. We knew the feeling......

We continued up a narrow channel where Jerry knew there was some nice bass. He now switched over to a small, electric, fishing motor that you controlled with your foot. You could sit in a comfortable chair, fish, control the motor's direction and speed with your foot, lean back and think it doesn't get any better than this. He began casting for bass. We watched him and were also enjoying watching some Canadian geese swim close by.

The water here was so clear that we watched bass swim out from under deadheads, and take his bait. Jerry caught 4 to 5 bass and returned everyone back to grow bigger.

After three hours on the water, we circled in, back to the dock. Cal had his fish in one hand and his fish pole in the other. He ran to find Grandma and showed her what he caught. "Next time, if we catch more, can we clean them and cook them up?" he asked. A lot of things happened that day. Cal caught his first fish. Jerry and I were privileged to re-see ourselves again catching our first fish through Cal, and a little boy became hooked on fishing, I think, for life.

...... "What we have done for ourselves alone dies with us; what we have done for others remains and is immortal" ......

Cal's first fish.

Chapter 22

Macho Benny and the Bear Hunt

I always thought that a hunter who hunted bear in the remote wilds by himself had to be a little "different", a little crazy, have a death wish, a real macho man, or all of the above.

I was in one of my favorite "watering holes" the other Friday. People were crowded in there for fish, fries and it seemed, just companionship. They all were looking to socialize and just get with other people after a long winter's confinement.

I met Benny, one of my old hunting friends that I hadn't seen for quite a while. "Ben," I asked, "Have you had any interesting hunting experiences lately?" Ben is about average height and normal weight. There was a guy with him that I would say was about 6 foot 2 and about 250 pounds. He looked like he could cut, peel, and carry out popple logs all day with no problem. His clothes rippled with muscles.

He carried himself like a guy that knew he was one-step tougher and caught the eye of the girls. He emptied his beer mug with one lift, wiped his mouth on his sleeve and smiled. He just knew people were watching and admiring him. He was getting free drinks from complete

strangers who "wanted to be sure" he knew they were on his side.
He'd drink, smile, ripple his muscles, and bask in the looks of approval coming his way. This guy gave you the feeling that he could handle himself and any two guys that challenged him.

Ben said, "We got a bear hunter story that you should like. I'll see if Marty (the big guy) will tell it to you." "Marty, will you tell Bob about your Canadian bear hunt this year?" Marty almost dropped his mug. He set it down on the bar......HARD! That big looking, macho guy seemed to be petrified and then wilted, like he suddenly saw a ghost!

"I'm never going bear hunting again!" said Marty. "Easy, Marty, easy, just relax and tell him the story of your hunt." explained Ben. Marty was visibly shaken. He looked all around, out the windows from where he was standing, checking for something.

He said, "Well, I'll tell you. I never thought I was afraid of bears. Here's what happened." (He seemed to suddenly become noticeably afraid.) "My hunting buddy, Ed and I, read about trophy bear hunts in the Misty Mountain area of Saskatchewan, Canada. They advertised that a guide goes with you to take care of your needs and guarantees you shoot at trophy sized bear."

"Ed and I dreamed of this trip for quite a while. It was described as thick timber country. The only humans around for miles were a few other bear hunters that were guided in there. We're both good shots with bows and arrows and this sounded really good to us, miles of wilderness…no main roads in there, only jeep trails cut by the guides."

Saskatchewan. Even the Province name sounded native. We were thinking back into time, Indian hunters with bows and arrows shooting huge trophy sized bear years ago. We would be like living history and have fun besides. We made the arrangements, paid our fees, and spent the first evening talking it over with our guide. He told us that he had bear bait piles located in this dense "bush" (as they called the woods). He said that he had nice platform tree stands, safety belts and openings cut so a hunter could get some good shots from these tree stands.

He explained that he would place us in two different tree stands about 80 acres apart. 80 acres in that "bush" might just as well have been "on the other side of a mountain". You couldn't see, walk, or travel through that dense woods for a distance of even 50 feet.

The next morning, just at daylight, we drove through some of the poorest excuses for roads that I was ever on. That 4-wheel drive jeep seemed to have one wheel off the ground most of the time as we rolled through the "bush". We were hanging onto our seats with one hand and trying to protect our bows and arrows with the other.

After what seemed like an hour of this, he stopped, motioned to not talk, whispered to me to use the climbers he had screwed into this tree with the stand high above. The stand appeared about 30 feet in the air. He said, "Marty, I'll let you off here. See the bait pile over there? Climb up, get into the safety harness and wait quietly. You should see at least a few bear. Don't shoot any small ones because I know there are some mighty big ones here. I can't stay with you as I'll drive about 80 acres from here to another good spot.

Your partner, Ed, will have that. I'll stay with him. When it gets dark, we'll come back here for you. Stand quiet and good luck." With that, he drove out of sight down a road that looked like he made it himself. No gravel or sight of any bulldozing that road. Only bent over saplings, grass, and broken tree branches that he drove through.

I climbed the tree, got into the safety harness, adjusted my bow and notched an arrow. I also felt on my hip for my Bowie knife. Hunters seem to always carry a knife twice the size that they need in wilderness places. I was no exception. I used it for skinning and it gave me an extra feeling of security. All was in place. It was quiet. No birds singing. No chipmunks running around. You felt like you truly were the only live thing there…waiting for a bear.

I finally was getting numb legs from standing and all that quiet was starting to get to me. You can imagine a lot of things when you are really alone……away from your buddies and……only with a bow and arrow. Then I started to hear brush cracking behind me, then, to the side of me. I got to admit, I was starting to unravel a little bit. The ad said a guide would be with you. Mine said that he'd be 80 acres away.

Brush was starting to move down below. The tops of saplings were wiggling like something big was coming through. I then saw something black moving toward the bait pile. The sun was starting to set and it wasn't perfect vision all over down there. In a heavy woods, it gets darker very early. Then a good-sized bear started to move toward the bait pile. It was a HUGE bear. I figured that I'd get one good shot before dark. I eased into position and let loose on a nice broadside shot. That bear growled, ran in a circle, stood up with that arrow sticking out of his belly (I must have shot low) like he was looking for whoever caused him that pain.

Another bear came out to the bait pile. Mine came over to my tree, smelled around, and started to climb up. I couldn't see past the platform that I was standing on but could hear him growl loudly as his claws scrapped onto the tree bark. I felt him hit the bottom of my platform. He'd seem to hit it a few times and it would push up a few inches and then settle back down. I was sweating and thinking of that ad, "And a guide will be sitting with you." This bear was mad, determined, and ran an easy 350-400 pounds. HE KNEW I WAS UP ON THAT PLATFORM! He'd reach up on the top with one paw and felt around. Once he swiped one of my boots. He started to shake the platform up and down again. It was secured pretty good to that tree. Thank God, he didn't notice those climbers on the back of the tree. The second bear was now standing on its hind legs and watching with interest. That one looked like it could weigh 600-700 pounds to me but you have to remember, I was starting to panic and hold on to that tree.

He kept swinging his paw above the platform. I kicked at it and he finally went down. I waited 'til he went back to the bait pile and then I half climbed and half slid down that tree. I ran as fast as I could following those jeep tracks. I only hoped that I'd find the jeep before complete darkness in. Scared? I never was so scared in all my life. I finally found Ed and the guide standing by the jeep. "We were just fixing to pick you up. Any luck? Your buddy, Ed here, got himself a real nice one." I sat down and told them the story. The guide said, "You saw a nice trophy bear. Will you come and hunt again? I told him, "Only if he sits in that tree with me."

The locals in the bar were listening and seemed to stop buying Marty drinks after that story.

Chapter 23

What Happened to our Rabbit Hunting?

In the '50's and '60's, one great sport in Menominee County, Michigan was rabbit hunting. My shotgun at that time was a single shot 16-gauge Hopkins and Allen. It was very dependable and taught you to really aim as you only had one shot when a rabbit ran by. This gem was well used before I bought it. Guns at that time probably went through 3-4 different owners and each of them used it for many years. Mine cost $2.00 at that time and I probably was the fourth owner.

My brother had more firepower. He had a five shot, 12-gauge Winchester pump shotgun. He either paid $10.00 or $15.00 for it. When you racked a second shell through the chamber, one had to really work that slide pump HARD as it was well worn.

A box of shells for either shotgun cost $1.50 at that time. That was no problem as you could trap a few muskrats and sell their hides for $1.50 each. We looked at shells as "free" because anyone could trap a muskrat.

We seemed to always have a beagle hound. They were natural and excellent rabbit hunters. Finding a good-sized cedar swamp on a weekend with no other hunters' tracks around it before us was easy. We'd let the beagle out of the car and quickly let it into that swamp before the dog stirred up the rabbit population.

Many times, two rabbits would come running out behind each other ahead of the dog. John, a good friend of mine, and an excellent hunter taught us to "shoot the second rabbit first. The first one will keep coming as it didn't see the second one fall." Some of those rabbits seemed experienced and smart. Two would come out, we'd shoot once, that first rabbit would keep looking ahead but seemed to be feeling around behind it with one paw to see if that second rabbit was still there. Who said these rabbits were slow thinkers? They had to be good to survive.

With the travel time from home, a good hunt seemed to start about 10:00 a.m. and continue to about 2:00 p.m. By that time, we two hunters would have our limits of rabbits. These were snowshoe (hares) rabbits. They could leap about 2-3 feet between jumps when the dog was chasing them around in the swamp. If they were far enough ahead of the dog, they'd run a ways, stop and listen, then run again. These gave you the best shots if you were in the right place as they came "whistling" through.

We never wasted many shells. A quick whistle on our part, the rabbit would stop dead in his tracks. That gave the best shot in the thick cedar swamps. John, as I mentioned before, had a black lab that would hunt anything except, thank goodness, deer. In a cedar swamp, it would trail a rabbit until it caught sight of it. Then it put on a burst of extra speed like a racehorse coming around the last bend.

He'd catch the rabbit himself. You'd hear a squeal and if you were quick, you'd have a rabbit before the dog had a lunch. Most "up north" farmers had some type of swamp on their land. They didn't mind if you'd hunt rabbits there. The only comment I can remember from one was that he didn't want anyone taking any Christmas trees.

One can only eat so many rabbits back home. There is only so many ways to prepare rabbit. We were always getting more rabbits than we could eat. Other than giving some away to neighbors, we'd feed frozen rabbit to the dogs. We had never known anyone who bought bagged dog food at that time. Table scraps, frozen rabbit and scraps from a butcher shop made up a dog's diet.

By now, we became owners of a rat-tailed spaniel dog. That dog would retrieve ducks and love to flush partridge. We figured if that black lab could chase rabbits, that spaniel would too if we took it out with the beagle enough.

It never happened. The spaniel would follow happily behind the column of hunters. When the beagle started barking "rabbit", it would run hard to catch up to the beagle. The only problem was if you were walking in front of it on the trail, it would run between your legs full tilt. Any unlucky hunter that had it run between his legs unsuspecting because it came from behind, would fly over backwards from a one foot wide dog running through a four inch space between your walking legs. This never even slowed it up.

Then after you'd shoot a rabbit, it would retrieve it and want to bury it in the snow. Again, you had to be quick to recover that rabbit. It never did quite get the idea of rabbit hunting.

What changed things so we no longer have rabbits to hunt? One thing, the cedar swamps were younger and thicker. There was plenty of food for them with popple and cedar logging. There were a lot of predators around at that time. Where you saw a lot of rabbit tracks in a swamp, you also saw coyote, fox, and bobcat tracks. They seemed to pick off a few but never really cleaned out a good rabbit swamp.

The aging forest seemed to be the most noticeable reason why the rabbit hunting is becoming a thing of the past. Biologists talk about cycles up and down in numbers, as a 10 year cycle period. For that to be true today, all conditions for the 10 years would have to be the same. The forest being cut over to an extreme today and not allowed the swamps to regenerate themselves. They grow up into brush other than cedar as the deer will nip off any new, low-growing cedar.

As John says, "I've seen more rabbits in the city today, like we used to see them in the woods." That's true. They thrive in backyard gardens, under bird feeders, handouts from families feeding them in backyards, and live in the small woodlots with a city where there is no hunting.

These are the cottontail rabbits. Very few people have rabbit dogs around here anymore. Hunting them is just a lot of good memories.

Chapter 24

Surviving a U.P. Turkey Hunt

There is a nice, friendly, small restaurant in our camp area. We go there periodically in the evenings to get the latest news on the area hunting and whatever else is new.

I went in there last Saturday night. The place was crowded and most of the booths were taken. Long tables are the second choice in there for sitting. The guy next to me at the table was big. Not an ounce of fat on him. He looked at me and then looked at the guy on the other side of him. We were all strangers to each other. He seemed to be "busting out", to talk to someone but no one was talking to him……a stranger from somewhere.

He had all the new camouflaged clothes on so I asked him if he was turkey hunting. "I'm glad you asked me that," he said. "I'm from Detroit. I came up here to hunt for four days, then I have to go back home. I hunt on a farmer's land where I hunted deer for the last four years. He feeds the turkeys so they hang around. I pay him for hunting there so he lets me hunt each year.

This year, he seemed a little different though. When I came this year and made some small talk with him to get more friendly-like and find out more about the turkeys there, he looked real hard at me and said, "Don't shoot no cows." Heck, I'm going out there for turkeys. When I told him I was from Detroit, he seemed to get jumpy. Not all of us are gangsters down there. You've got to be tough to survive though.

Now, going into a small, backwoods establishment is a good place to learn what's what with the current hunt. That is, if you listen rather than do all the talking. This guy said that he read a lot of books on turkey hunting and how to successfully get one. He told me that you have to find where they roost and where they eat. Then, you sit somewhere's between those places with a nice hen decoy and do your turkey calling.

He said, "The farmer told me where they roost and where he feeds them. So, the next day, I was out there before daylight to be placed in the dark so I wouldn't scare any birds. The weather was cold with a little rain and snow mixed. When I pulled into the farmyard, the farmer was standing near where I parked my car. I said Hi to him and told him that I felt lucky."

He stared into my eyes and said, "Don't shoot no cows." What a dork. He must have thought that I didn't know what a cow was. I'll tell you, coming from Detroit, I'm not afraid of much. I put out my decoy and fixed a quick and comfortable blind in front of me. I was sitting with my back resting on two trees. My camouflaged clothes blended in well. I had on my camo hat with this rim all around it and two turkey feathers sticking in the back of it. I just bought a new shotgun for this trip. It's chambered for 3 ½ inch shells. All they had to do was come close.

I started calling and didn't get any answer. After doing this for about a half an hour, the sun was just coming up.

I could sense something behind me! I tried to turn my head so I could see behind. At the same moment, a big timber wolf was running up to bite me! (I later figured it saw those turkey feathers in my cap as I'd move my head back and forth.) He wasn't just sizing me up but he was making his attack! I only had time to smash him on the nose with the butt of my gun. At the same time, another timber wolf ran right past me from about five feet away! They were moving in for the kill. They ran away fast but I was shaking for ½ and hour after. No turkeys showed in the area. Heading back to the farm, I told the farmer about the wolves and no turkeys.

He said, "The wolves can be a problem but there are turkeys out there. He started smelling me. I thought that was odd. "You smell different coming from Detroit. Those turkeys can smell a different smell like yours and shy away from it. Why don't you hang your clothes in the barn overnight? You'll smell like a cow tomorrow but they are used to that smell and your chances of seeing one should be better." I did that and he was right. I really did smell like a cow. My car now smells like a cow......and I still didn't see any turkeys."

I left that hunter and went back to my camp to spend the night and to fight the "lady bugs." If you live rural, you know what I'm talking about with the "lady bug" problem. All I have to do in early spring is heat up my camp and they appear from nowhere. They crawl all over the windows but also fly into everything. I visited an old bachelor friend that lives up near the camp. I pulled up into his yard with my pickup as he was just coming out the door to see who it was. "Hi Al," I said, "He answered, "Lady bug, lady bug, damned old lady bugs." He had more lady bugs in there than anyone deserved.

They not only were getting to him, they GOT him! He'd keep saying, "Lady bug, lady bug" when you talked to him. I left shortly after.

I met my friend, Pinto, the next day. Pinto's got a camp up near mine. I don't know where he got that name, Pinto, and it seems like none of his friends know or care either. Everyone just calls him Pinto.

He was all happy and told me that he shot a nice big, Tom Turkey yesterday. He said, "The things you don't see in the woods are a wonder. I just sat down to hunt when I heard a rabbit squealing in the swamp next to me. You could tell some other animal had caught it and was slowly killing it. After a while, it stopped squealing. I quietly walked down where I heard it and saw a beautiful, colored, bobcat eating that rabbit. It seen me and disappeared. I checked the rabbit and only the two hind quarters were still left. I went back to my turkey blind (just a cushion against a big tree with some brush in front of me.) I sat there quietly for about 30 minutes and then saw movement coming towards me. That bobcat was coming back and it had two other bobcats with it. They all seemed to be a good size. What you don't see when you don't have a camera."

I was thinking, those turkeys have to survive bobcats, weasels, wolves, coyotes, fox, eagles, fishers, and who knows what else. Then a sportsman tries his luck with trying to get one. I saw the guy from Detroit again the next day in Stephenson, a small town near our camp. He said that he wasn't going turkey hunting alone again. Those wolves unnerved him. He claimed that he'd bring a partner on the next trip so they could sit back to back and no wolves could surprise them. I asked, "What does that farmer say about you bringing more people in to hunt?" The guy kind of looked off into space for a while, then said, "You know, the only thing he said was, 'Don't shoot no cows.'"

Chapter 25

Spring Life, at the Camp

The snow is fast disappearing in the woods. At camp, you can see the deer starting to move around on the highland, moving slow and grazing on grass under the evergreen trees. Our neighbor's camp put out corn for them and already they have an unwanted bear coming and visiting.

The neighbors are starting to make maple syrup. It reminds me of when my two sons were 10 and 12 years old. They drilled holes and hung cans on about 25 trees by our camp to collect sap. They tapped pine, birch, maple and a variety of other trees. We went home after that weekend at camp before there was any to collect. The next weekend, the maple cans were empty. Either the squirrels or the deer drank that sweet sap.

The boys quickly forgot about that project after they learned that sap from birch and pine trees wasn't "too sweet," and they saw a porcupine high up in a tree near the camp. They shot at it with their BB guns from almost ½ day. Those BB's hardly had the velocity to reach that high. Once in a while that porcupine would stop eating, look down at them like it was a little annoyed, and move up higher about six inches.

That was the start of two "would be" sportsmen coming back excited and telling how they shot a porcupine but it was too "afraid" to fall down. Then we went to visit two bachelors that lived in a "real" log cabin about five miles from our camp. Their names were Andy and June. June, an odd name for a man, but they were really "unique" individuals anyway. Nothing bothered them and they showed very little emotion.

My boys would enjoy chasing the mice around on the floor in their cabin as they would suddenly streak by. The kids would run behind them and try to step on one. Andy and June evidently weren't bothered by the mice either. My boys were all excited and had a hard time waiting for another one to streak by.

The conversation from Andy and June seemed to be, "How much wood do you think we need to cut today?" They would cut enough firewood for one day at a time and "just enough" for that day. From the deep thinking that they were doing, they must have cut different amounts for different days, depending upon the temperature.

After a while, my boys asked them were their TV was? They said, "We had one, but it blew out." My boys looked at them in amazement. In town, if your TV blew out, you'd buy another one......not just forget about it.

When I think about it, these guys had no daily or weekly newspaper, no working radio, or other "outside" communications to even know the news. The country could be at war and they would have no idea, although, it probably wouldn't make any difference to them anyway. Once in a while, one of them would walk into our camp with a small pot and ask for some live coals from the stove. Their fire would go out from not putting more wood in it on time and they would use these live coals to re-start the fire. I can remember once after they left, one of the boys said, "Why didn't we just give them some matches?" I thought about it for a while and said, "Hey, if they want coals, we'll give them coals."

June was saying, "The refrigerator don't work anymore either but we use the shelf space in it. He smiled and said, "That's one place that the mice can't get into." My boys just looked at each other and seemed to open their eyes twice as wide.

These were the same two guys that, a few years ago, were visited by the members of Camp North Star, another deer camp in our area. The bachelors treated them to some freshly baked bread that they just took out of the oven. Red, from that camp, told me later, "That bread smelled so good in with a pound of fresh, government surplus, butter. We ate it and it seemed to melt in your mouth, it tasted so good. Red even complimented them on the caraway seed that they put in it. He said they were good but they tasted sweet.

Andy slowly turned and looked at his brother. "Those mice must have got into the flour again." Red and his camp crew left quickly and tried to wash down that "caraway seed" back at their camp. This was the time of the year that we had our annual smelt fry at the camp. We opened both top windows on each end of the camp, turned on the ceiling fans and let the smoke roll as we fry up about 10 pounds of smelt on the wood kitchen stove.

115

That meal is followed some weekend later by making homemade potato pancakes with homemade maple syrup. This is also a "smoky" meal to cook on the wood kitchen stove. They must be good because it's hard for the cook to keep ahead of the "eaters". They even ate them off of the serving plate on the "Dutch Oven" above the wood stove before they can reach the table. The last big meal is the venison fry.

Then there is riding on the 4-wheeler at camp. There is a magic formula for young boys: A 4-wheeler, mud, being young, mud, a challenge to see if you can go through it without getting stuck, more mud and very, very, muddy young boys. They come back to camp with both the 4-wheeler and themselves looking like they just applied a heavy coat of natural camouflage to the 4-wheeler and to themselves.

Spring, fresh air, good company, and traditional meals, that's what spring camp life is about at our camp.

U.P. Humor:

Children were lined up in the cafeteria of a Catholic school for lunch. At the head of the table was a large pile of apples. The nun made a note, "take only one, God is watching."

Moving through the line, at the other end of the table was a large pile of chocolate chip cookies. A boy wrote a note, "take all you want, God is watching the apples."

Chapter 26

Our Camp Knew No Hero's

The regular hunting crew was up to our deer camp last October doing the routine chores for the coming deer season. Cutting, splitting, putting firewood in the shed, repairing deer blinds and making new ones at better looking locations.

On the way to camp, on the last gravel road in, Carl saw five timber wolves walk across the road. "Two very big ones and three smaller ones," according to Carl. After a camp supper, the conversations switched over to those wolves. "How tall were they, Carl?" "Did they look like they could take down a man?"

Carl thought a while and then said, "Guys, I wouldn't have wanted to be outside of my truck by that bunch. They walked off the road just far enough so you couldn't see them. Then I could see one eye looking at me through the brush. I then saw another one with both eyes looking at me from behind a tree. I'll never forget those eyes. They were scary. Talk about a fearless stare from an animal. Pound for pound I don't think a man would be any match for a full grown one without a weapon."

Now everyone was talking about building a better deer blind for themselves. 2" x 4" frames with solid plywood sheeting, small windows, and a solid door should make us feel comfortable again," Bob said.

"That tent blind isn't TOO bad," Bill said. "It's got stakes attaching it tightly to the ground and a zip shut door. I feel comfortable in that." Vic, who sits in the shed and has an open window with one side missing on the shed started to nervously shift in his chair. He likes to fall asleep out there and now he has to worry about more than the mice running over him.

Tim started to laugh. "You know, this reminds me of that story about the 'Three Little Pigs'. One had a stronger house, one had a normal house and one had a weak one. And.........the wolf was after THEM too!"

Now this season, no one seems to stay out too late so they have to walk in during the dark. We had a copy of yesterday's paper. It said that Michigan's UP has 408 wolves in 86 packs. Carl was just reading this out loud. "I think I heard two packs from my post yesterday. One pack was north of me and the other was about ½ mile west. Bill, I'll give you the tent blind tomorrow. Lots of deer sign over there." Bill just smiled.

The deer hunt was on......Cousin Tim, our in-house Pastor, just finished blessing our breakfast gruel. The excitement for going out for deer before daylight was wearing off. There was a noticeable, gloomy, mood setting in. It was still raining from an all night rain. It rained yesterday too. Nothing was moving outside and it appeared that the no-bucks-so-far guys didn't want to go out either.

Carl said, "That portable outhouse blind that we bought this year could work as a huge umbrella. I'm going to get

inside of it and carry it to a good deer trail and post."
"Good idea." Dave said. "Try to stay out to at least two
o'clock. They might start moving early." Pushing his
chair away from the table, Dave said, "What are we
going to have for dinner?" "Some of that good 5 day old
sauerkraut casserole." "Don't that stuff have hair on it?"
muttered Dave? "Easy on the sauerkraut, Carl. I'm so
full of gas from that, I'm starting to sound like my .308 in
the woods." "Looks like another all day rain," Bob said.
"But we have choices. We can play cards, sleep, or we
could go to the Casino." "Let's go to the Casino," said
Vic. "Someone should go out and bait our deer blinds,"
Bill said. NO one moved on either of those thoughts.
There's something about an all day, gentle rain. It
relaxes you and has the most pleasant sound of the roof.

We'll know it's time to go out again when we hear those
wolves hollering. They don't like to hunt in the rain
either." Sleep won out as the best choice. A nice wood
heater fire crackling and thumping as the wood burned
and dropped to the bottom of the heater. That sometimes
gentle rain changing to sudden downpours on the camp
roof. What pleasurable sounds in a nice, warm cabin.
No one had to "answer the clock" as when we were
home.

The camp became silent except for the rain, the sounds
from the wood heater, and an occasional "toot" from
someone that ate that sauerkraut hot dish.

Chapter 27

Are Deer Getting Smarter?

We've hunted the same land in Menominee County, Michigan for at least 40 years. We've enjoyed good hunting seasons and a few poor ones. We shift around a bit but we basically hunt the same lands.

Bill, Hoover, John and I make up the camp roster for most of those seasons. All are good compatible guys. We shared most everything at camp. Hoover's real name is Cliff. Everyone called him Hoover after the vacuum cleaner as, when he'd eat, he'd suck in all food within his reach. He always wanted to cook. The first dinner meal he made consisted of beans, rutabagas, greasy bacon, and tainted canned milk for the coffee. Everyone ate a lot and then got diarrhea the next morning.

No one hunted the next day. It was like a "cleaning out day" from the meal. This particular year, the Wisconsin season started a week later than the Michigan season. Our hunting grounds bordered the Menominee River. This river was the boundary line between Michigan and Wisconsin. We always saw big bucks in this area. They are not the easiest to get a shot at, however. You'd see them at a distance, or see them jump over a single land road. They seemed to be very smart bucks.

These bucks stayed within range of the Menominee River and at the first sound of gunshots on the Michigan side, would swim over to the Wisconsin side into the safety of the yet closed season there.

At daybreak on the first day of the season this year, there were six cars parked along what we call the "Conservation Road." The DNR made this road to open up the State's 40's in that area for hunting. Just at daybreak, there was shooting up and down the road steady from 7:30 a.m. to 9:30 a.m. Then I could hear deer running our way through the woods. All of a sudden, there was loud and continuous splashing into the water.

Deer were jumping into the river and splashing upwards until it looked like the water was boiling. Six deer were making their way over to the Wisconsin "safe" side of the river. We hunted hard and didn't see any more deer. I saw three deer come down to the riverbank to get a drink. They then walked peacefully up the riverbank into the woods. This was on the Wisconsin side, of course. Animals are smart. Have you ever had to sneak up on a duck along a riverbank? They fly at the first snap of a stick. That same duck, in a city limits, will eat alongside of a river and stay there all day. The city noise doesn't bother them. They seem to KNOW where they are safe.

Another time, I was driving our old "camp car" back out of the one-lane wood's road. I was posting for deer since sun up that day and now was cold. Three doe jumped across the road about 30 feet in front of me. I stopped the car, shut it off, and took my rifle out of its case. After loading, I rested it on a tree limb for complete steadiness.

Thinking a buck would be behind those does, I waited a good 20 minutes. Nothing. So, I cleared the gun of shells, placed it back in its case and started the car. That car just started up and a big, 10-point buck walked across the road, into the woods and out of sight.

Another lesson in deer hunting: Always take your rifle to the outhouse. A couple of seasons ago, one of our camp members, Bill, went to the outhouse at about noon. The door faces away from the camp and sitting in there, faces the woods. We normally leave the door open on it as, it then lets in more light and the view is beautiful facing the wooded ridge just in front of it.

Bill could hear someone walking to the outhouse through the dry leaves all around there. Moments later, a huge 10-point buck walked about 30 feet in front of him. He said, "It never knew I was there and it looked like he was on the trail of some female companionship. A 10-pointer is a rare sighting. Had he had his gun with him, he would have most likely have gotten it.

We did see a lot less deer this season than normal. Everywhere in the U.P. where we know other hunters said the same thing. People talked about the "harsh winter" having an effect on the number of deer. How about the wolf population? They have to eat all year round. How many deer do they consume? There is no regulation on their number at all.

Maybe a trapping or hunting season on them may be necessary to preserve the deer population. Other than having deer for hunting, motels, taverns, restaurants, sports equipment stores, and land rental all depend upon a healthy deer herd economy in the U.P. Wolf population helps no one when they become overpopulated.

Just when you think that you have deer patterns figured out, they pull something for survival. A month before season, we studied out the deer trails, where they made a few tracks down into the water for drinking, where their "beds" were evident alongside of ridges and how many seemed to be in the area.

We were going by visual sightings of deer to count them. No DNR counting methods for us. Like, count the deer pellets, check them for size, divide by 12, as it was written that they relieved themselves by 12's; then cover a 100 feet square area. Take a total count in this area with the above formula and multiply it times the number of 100 feet sections where you hunt. That should tell you how many deer passed your way over a 3-day period. There, of course, are a few flaws in this arrangement. Some deer may not get the urge and waltz right on through without dropping anything. Some smart old buck may see you counting pellets and let 40-50 fly, just to mix up your count.

From the fresh and well-used trails, we knew we were in good spots to see deer. Closer to November 15th, we baited with your average corn, apples, carrots, cabbage, pumpkins, and a few potatoes. Deer were visiting our bait piles regularly. On occasion, we thought we could hear some of them passing gas from probably eating too much cabbage. That is a dead give-a-way to where they are hiding.

We felt that we were dealing with smarter than average deer back here. One, it was a long way back from any road where a regular hunter could drive to. Two, from what we observed these deer had big horns meaning they lived longer than their cousins with the small horns on easy-to-get-to sections.

Carl commented, "This should be a good year for us. We know they're here, they're big, and we've got them boxed in along the river." We had deer blinds on three sides with the river on the fourth side acting, we felt, like a fence to keep them coming right to our posts.

Dave said, "Boys, we've got it made. We got choice blinds, we baited well, lots of deer, and we're ready. The hay is in the barn......Yes sir, WE'VE GOT IT MADE!" He always had a way with words and says stuff like that.

Opening Day! We were all up at 4:45 a.m. We washed up, dressed, and got ready for a good old camp breakfast; bread, eggs, greasy bacon, tainted milk for the coffee, as someone forgot to put it back in the refrigerator, and leftover sauerkraut. We were all at our posts before full daylight. The sun was rising and "lighting up" the tops of the trees. It slowly was creeping down to the tree trunks and then to the ground. What a beautiful sight!

Sounds echoed up and down the river. It was like a cattle stampede in a western movie. These deer were no dummies. They somehow KNEW that there was no shooting on the Wisconsin side (that season opens a week later than Michigan). The water was churned into foam as they crossed.

The second week, we were posted in the same placed when the Wisconsin hunters opened up. It sounded like a small war for a while. Then, as if on cue, a herd of deer jumped into the river from the Wisconsin side and swam over to the Michigan side. We didn't get any of those as they looked like either, does, cripples, and walking wounded. The smart bucks probably crossed after dark.

We headed back to camp after one day's hunt in the second week. The guys wanted to "go to town" (Stephenson) to eat and I believe just to see people.

One old timer in the restaurant was saying, "Ya, after the first day, no one saw any bucks where we hunt. I do believe that after one day, the bucks unscrewed their horns and hid them under a stump for the rest of the deer season."

"I wonder," Carl thought. "That guy may be right."

To those in North Dakota, Minnesota, Wisconsin, and for that matter the rest of the country, I must report the Sad News that Ole was SHOT. He was up by the Canadian border on his 4-wheeler cutting some trees, when some rangers looking for terrorists spotted him. According to the news reports, using a loudspeaker, they shouted to him, "Who are you and what are you doing?" Ole shouted back,

"OLE......BIN LOGGIN!"

Ole is survived by his wife Lena and Lena's good friend Lars.

Chapter 28

Riding Low in the Water

Four of us were making a fly-in fishing trip into the Canadian wilderness. We started out from home with way too much equipment to meet the safe weight limit on this loaded plane. I could tell by looking at the huge pile as each one of us loaded it into the van that we would ride to Canada in. Man, that pile was BIG, compared to a regular year.

Bob said, "Don't worry, we can bribe the guy on the dock weighing our stuff with a Canadian beer. Give him a can when he starts to weigh it." We arrived at the dock and find two new guys doing the dock work (weighing) rather than "oiled up" Al.) We try the beer bribe and they both turned it down. That's the first time we encountered a Canadian woodsman that turned down a beer. (Al always said, "If you put the cases of pop and beer on your laps when you fly, I'll count that as 'carry-on baggage' like the airliners do.") I never could quite figure out how the plane knew the difference of where you carried it. Weight was weight.

The pilot did tell us some trips ago, that year's before they started to weigh the freight, that he would roar across the lake on the take-off and if it didn't lift off of the water by a certain spot that he watched from the shoreline, he'd cut the throttle then go back and unload some items and do it again.

These two "dockhands" would weigh a large scale full of items, then pile it to the left of the scale. The items left to weigh was on its right. We were allowed 400 pounds of baggage (groceries, fishing gear, sleeping bags, and yes, beer comes under groceries.) We had to diplomatically say no to many items that some of the guys wanted to take from home as, fish finders and their heavy batteries, binoculars, extra boat seat cushions, and this and that.

The weight limit was adding up close on that scale and we still had a sizable pile to go. Bill saw his heavy boots left to weigh so he put them on. They didn't weigh people, only baggage. Strange, as I'm sure the plane couldn't tell the difference of where the weight was coming from.

The "dockhand" said, "Take some of this stuff and put it back in your van. Think priorities. You don't need it all. I suppose you guys even took a change of underwear for each day too." I noticed Dave started to smell the dockhand. I suppose he was wondering how many days he got out of a pair of underwear that he was wearing.

Someone normally thinks of a way to work things out. The dockhand would step over 10 feet and look what we put back in the van. At the same time, someone would take some of the overweight items, bypass the scale and put them on the already weighed pile.

The dockhand said, "It looks like your doing alright. There's not much left to weigh." I look up at the sky, whistled a bit and walked away. We successfully got the whole load on except one pair of hip boots which were only planning to pull through a water channel into another lake and keep us dry this year.

We all got into the plane and the pilot said, "You guys must have gained weight this year.
We're riding lower in the water. (The plane's pontoons were almost all under water) John asked him, "Do you have the pontoons pumped out?" "We've got new pontoons this year and they don't leak," countered the pilot. "Don't worry," he said. "I'll run the whole lake to take off. Once we're airborne, it flies easy." (Normally. we would only need ½ of the lake for a runway take off) He revved up the motor to an ear piercing sound. We all had been given earplugs but it still was loud. Then he pulled back on the throttle......hard! We leaped sluggishly forward. He pulled back still more on that throttle. We were now racing toward the far tree lined shore across the lake.

Normally, when we run ½ the lake, the plane starts to rise for the take off. This trip, it just roared faster and faster, toward the other rock infested, tree lined shore. Our pilot was young. He didn't even look like he shaved yet. I was hoping he knew what all those levers and switches were for on the dashboard. That far shore was coming up FAST!!

One of our guys panicked and screamed above the roar of the motor, "Let's go back and unload some WEIGHTTTTTTT!" At that point, we broke loose from the water, cleared the trees by about 20 feet (they sure looked close!) and was airborne. A trip like this will clear your mind of any work related problems back at home. The pilot smiled and said, "It's like playing football. One yard can give you a touchdown. One yard here can set you free, as long as you clear the trees." No one falls asleep on our plane trips.

Bill took Dramamine pills to prevent airsickness. He never had it but he didn't want it either. I don't know how many he took but he was like a zombie when we helped him down from the plane. After about 40 minutes of rough flying, we landed on our lake, taxied to the dock, unloaded and carried all of our possessions up to the camp. How come all cabins seem UP somewhere? We always carry everything uphill.

The pilot then started up the motor and was soon disappearing into the sky. The last sound of that motor left us in complete isolation for a week. Now is the time when you walk extra careful, watch where you step, and get into the boat with a little more care than you would back home.

The guys carried the boats into the water, picked out a good motor and filled up the gas tanks. There are always four motors at camp to use on two boats. One never will work. Two seem to work perfectly and one makes a good spare. You have to guess which is going to be which as they are different each year.

We were fishing within ½ hour, lots of enthusiasm but not many fish biting. We are averaging about one fish per hour on that first day. There were speckled trout. The lake was capable of having 20-inch "specks" in it from years past. We did catch enough for a fish fry that night. The next day and night, it rained steady. It rained so hard, you couldn't see across the lake. Then there was a very loud cracking sound outside the camp. In this strong wind, a huge tree about 3 feet thick and 150 feet long uprooted itself and crashed between the cabin and the outhouse. Ten feet more to the west and one wall of the camp plus roofing could have very well collapsed too. We were now approximately 75 air miles for the nearest road.

Don said, "You know guys, I forgot to bring any changes of underwear." Jerry said, "That's OK. You can change with Bill and he change with you." Everyone got a laugh out of that except Don.

We fished the best spots that we knew with minimum results. Then on the last day, one of our boats fished what we always felt was the shallow end of the lake, "Instant success". They caught fish one on each pole and at the same time many times. Then they called our boat over and we all caught A LOT of fish! These were BIG fish!! 16 to 19 inches were common. Some looked like they were pushing four pounds.

We concluded that they were beginning to spawn. These were huge fish to be in such shallow water. The gravel bottom was perfect for trout spawning. Everyone was catching fish. A loon was working a shore area near us and surfaced with a fish. We later saw a bear on the far side of the lake where we took the fish heads and innards so we hoped no bear would come by the cabin. There also was a mink darting in and out between the racks on the shore carrying a small fish in its mouth.

Moose tracks were fresh on the shore but we didn't see any moose. Wah! The size of those moose tracks!! The tangle foot that they travel through showed that they have to be one huge animal.

Don said, "We could live off of the land up here. I saw some edible mushrooms, enough for a big meal, some wintergreen berries, and a lot of blueberries." We did have a big meal of mushrooms and later, some blueberry pancakes. The guys were literally scraping their plates after those meals.

We had so many fish fries that it seemed we had to force them down toward the end. Just think so many brook trout (speckled trout) that you got sick of eating them! Everyone pushed their chairs away from the table and the stories started. John said, "Did Bill tell you about him taking pictures of a bear in his yard?" He told me that he saw bear poop by his broken bird feeder. He then bought one of those night cameras that you set up to see what comes by your deer post at night. He set it up then went back and finished cutting his grass. The next day, he checked and all 12 pictures were used up in the camera. He took the film in to be developed and the next day got them back. On his pictures, he has 12 pictures of himself cutting grass from 12 different angles."

Good friends, good fishing, a real wilderness trip. I'm sure everyone's blood pressure dropped back to a low normal from all of the relaxation and shared experiences. These memories will soon be set aside too, because of the fast approaching deer season. This same crew deer hunts so it should be interesting. We'll have to tell Bill not to wave at the camera if he sets it up by his deer blind.

A Fisherman's wife gave birth to twin boys. When the babies were side by side, they always looked in opposite directions, so they were named Forward and Away. Years later the fisherman took his sons fishing, but they didn't return.

Months passed, and the wife finally spotted her husband plodding sadly up the beach. He explained to her that during their trip, Forward had hooked an enormous fish. He had struggled for hours, when suddenly the fish pulled Forward into the water and they never saw him again. "That's just terrible!" his wife said.

"It was terrible all right," said the fisherman. "But you should have seen the one that got Away!"

Chapter 29

How Cold Was It?

A real Yooper doesn't mind a little cold weather. We've been spoiled over the last few years with the above normal temperatures that we have been having. In fact, the whole first week of deer season this year, the temperature was in the 50's.

There was hardly any snow for people with snowmobiles. A good 4 wheeler could be used the year round now. So, this weekend, when "Escanaba Johnny" called and wanted to go to the camp for a few days, we thought nothing of it. Our camp is insulated and we've got a good wood supply piled high on the porch and little snow to drive through to get to the camp.

On a normal year, we'd have to find a "friendly" to plow us out. Mid-January should have at least 2 feet of snow on the level. John said, "We'll have it made. We can drive in easy, start the fires, go to the casino where it's warm, and come back to a warm camp." We wanted to catch a ride on the casino bus. They give "perks" for riding it, as, $20.00 free money to spend and points to earn for free meals.

Because we started late, we just got to the bus pick up spot on time and didn't go to camp early to "start the fires" as we intended. The pickup truck was running good so we saw no problems. How long could it take to heat up the camp? The last time that we were up there was the last week of deer season in November. We had a lot of good memories floating around in our heads from then.

The casino bus brought us back to our truck at about 11:15 p.m. We returned poorer but wiser men. I said, "We'll get THEM next time. I figured out more ways of playing that blackjack game now." Johnny was staring straight ahead. "Ya," he said. "We can't keep losing FOREVER! Our luck has GOT to change. Did you see that little old lady with the "win" trough full of money? I'm thinking that she must have been a "plant" by the casino to motivate the rest of us to spend more." "I don't think so," I said. "I saw a little old man grab up the winnings and they both went out the door. I watched their car leave and slip and slide all over highway 41."

Our truck radio now announced that the wind chill is at 25° below zero. "If there are no trees down across the camp road, we'll have it made." John sounded so positive. Our single lane camp road goes in for the distance of 40 acres. It would be no picnic if we had to get out in the cold to move trees. We made it in with no problem. Four wheel drive, a few "Hail Mary's" and there was nothing to it. Strange how John gets so religious when we're in a pinch, I thought. He seldom goes to church.

We sat up until 3:30 in the morning while the fires blazed. They seemed to make a very slow affect on warming anything up in camp. My wife said before I left home. "Whatever you do, don't sleep on those cold mattresses until they warm completely up or you'll get

134

pneumonia." I thought that over and figured that I'd let Johnny try one first. Then, as I was leaving the house, she says, "By the way, is your insurance paid up?" A wife's way of telling you, you're probably nuts for going up there in 25° below zero weather but be careful.

"I don't mind sitting up on these wooden chairs so long, do you John?" I asked. (The wooden kitchen chairs had no padding and heated up relatively fast.) "Not a bit," John said trying not to chatter his teeth. I wonder if we could sleep on these if we leaned against an inside wall?"

About 3:30 a.m., we went to sleep sitting up on the sofa located near the big wood heater. "Laying down sleeping is just a state of mind. We'll never know the difference after we fall asleep with all of these heavy blankets on us. Look, you can't even see your breath in here anymore." Things are looking up. Even at 25° below zero, its nice being up to the camp.

The next day, we saw five deer go across the backyard. They looked in very good shape. The little amount of snow in the woods is a plus for them. They can move around on the high land finding food. The timber wolves are a little less of a threat to them as they won't be bogged down in deep snow.

John said, "Did I tell you about that timber wolf that I saw by my camp last year?" (His camp is northwest of Escanaba.) "I was walking down my camp road and I saw it standing off to the side and watching me. It was about 40-50 feet away. It stared into my eyes and I stared back. Animals watch your eyes to see if you're afraid. I raised my arms up above my head to look taller to scare it away, and it immediately stepped about four steps

135

TOWARDS ME! Then I jumped up and down, hollering and waving my arms. It slowly turned, walked away, stopped and looked back at me about 3-4 times before it disappeared into the woods. That thing must have weighed between 200 and 250 pounds. I know, because he looked about the size of my brother-in-law when he gets down on all fours to look into the refrigerator.

Then we started our old debate all over again. Why did the DNR recently plant those wolves in the U.P.? We were happier without them. They eat a lot of deer and must hunt year round, not just the 15-day season like we do. The deer hunts put a lot of money into the U.P. economy. (Hunters buy food, lodging, deer bait, lease land, pay taxes, just to hunt deer.) The wolves add nothing.

Dirtying dishes the next morning meant that we had to wash them and carry water in from the pump in 25° below zero weather. It wasn't long and we were heading into town for breakfast. Now, that restaurant was an experience. It was REALLY cold in there. Either the thermostat didn't work or whoever was supposed to "fire up" got up late. How cold was it? The first clue in there was one waitress had earmuffs on. It looked like another waitress mixed some anti-freeze into her spray bottle of water to wash the tables. It was the right color for that too.

One customer wanted a piece of pie. The waitress was banging that pie tin on the counter trying to get its frozen cover off. That piece of pie was so beat up that it looked like it fell on the floor when she served it. No one complained so they must have been used to that.

The main waitress, Judy, didn't want to talk. Normally, you can't keep her quiet. She said she had a split lip from the cold temperatures and didn't want it to break open. She had her jacket on and the other one looked like she wished that she did.

The owner was the cook. She told me that the waitresses were hard to get in this cold weather. One had whooping cough and the other had diarrhea. We got the one with the whooping cough. How cold was it? One customer went to the restroom, washed his hands but didn't dry them completely. His had became glued to the outside door knob when he left. They had to pour warm water on it to set him free. I heard someone say, "Someone shut the door!" Another said, "How can you tell when it's shut?"

People seem to adjust to most everything. I heard a couple of guys talking as they were warming their hands on their coffee cups. "We sure are lucky here. We don't get those floods, mud slides, or big car accidents like other parts of the country." "If we could just get that DNR to admit their mistake with stocking all those wolves up here, we could fix that." Another said, "That would be like President Bush admitting we didn't have to go to war with Iraq because they had no weapons of mass destruction. Now, he wants to "adjust" Social Security to save us money. I wonder what scare he'll tell the people like he did with Iraq to screw up the Social Security? Do you realize if young people invest their money privately instead of keeping all of it flowing in Social Security, it would short-change the monies available to keep it smooth flowing for those people on it?" If they were right or wrong, that was pretty deep thinking for such cold weather. Then I heard someone on the other side of the restaurant say, "What are you complaining about the cold for? At least we don't have any mosquitoes!"

BOB HRUSKA'S OTHER BOOKS AVAILABLE:

Quantity   **Cost**

_____ *Humorous Stories From the U.P.*
Hunting Camps Vol. 1($10.00 Postage Paid) _____

_____ *Humorous Fishing Stories From*
the U.P. Vol. 2 ($10.00 Postage Paid)   _____

_____ *More, Humorous Hunting Camp Stories*
Vol. 3 ($10.00 Postage Paid)   _____

_____*Planned Danger Vol. 4 (These are more*
dangerous hunt/fish humorous experiences)
($10.00 Postage Paid)   _____

_____ *Hilarious Hunting, Camp and Fishing Stories*
Vol. 5 ($10.00 Postage Paid)   _____

If you like Patrick McManus, You will love Bob Hruska's excitement and humor. These stories may bring back similar experiences that you can relate to. Most are guaranteed to make you laugh. Some are said to have lowered high blood pressure.

Special!! If you buy the entire series, you will save 10% or $1.00 off per book (if ordered directly from author).

To order: Make a copy of this form and send to: Robert R Hruska, Author, 140 S Birch Ave, Gillett, WI 54124.

ORDER INFORMATION NEEDED:

NAME_____

ADDRESS_____

CITY_____STATE_____ZIP_____
Make checks payable to: Robert R. Hruska, Author